It's Never THAT Simple

ESSAYS TO BROADEN THE CONVERSATION

It's Never THAT Simple

ESSAYS TO BROADEN
THE CONVERSATION

John D. Powell, Ph.D.

ISBN: 978-0-578-55356-6

Layout & Cover Design by Tinyah M. Hawkins

Published by IngramSpark

Printed in the USA - justenoughlight.com

IN APPRECIATION

I have many to thank. First and foremost, my wife, Judy, has played a huge role in these opinion articles. She has been my primary encouragement to write, and she has been my sounding board for ideas and tone. I generally give her my second or third draft to read. By then I have whittled away much of the fluff and gotten the article closer to the 750-word limit. My instructions to her are simple. First, "See if it holds together and makes the point." I don't want the writing to be rambling or going in too many directions and never getting anywhere. Second, "Let me know if it's too hostile." I write about issues that are important to me, and I tend to get worked up as I write. She is usually the one who lets me know when my aggravation is getting in the way of the point I'm trying to make.

I email copies to people I know are of like mind. I need their support and challenge just as much as I need the dissenting opinions. I am grateful to the Bold Type book group. They always affirm my efforts, they have shared some of the articles with their college classes, and they encouraged me to get this book in print. I have some friends I see regularly, like Mark and Don and Charlie, who never fail to thank me for my words and challenge me with their ideas. Over an IPA, Ray routinely pushed my thinking as much as anyone. He applauded and challenged me in every conversation. Then he died suddenly a year ago. I miss his depth and compassion, and I frequently ask myself, "What would Ray say about this?" Also in the background stand my four brothers who over the years have done as much as anyone to help me think more deeply, spiritually, and inclusively. These and many other friends and former colleagues have been important in this process, and through these essays I want them to know who I am now.

INTRODUCTION

This book is a collection of essays printed by the Abilene Reporter News in their Sunday opinion section. When I submitted my first opinion article in 2007, I was nervous. That first article, "The War on Christmas," was far from scandalous, but I thought it might be on the edge for Abilene, a politically and religiously conservative city. I made the argument that this "war" was not waged by liberals, but was merely noise by conservative Christians angered that their previously unfettered privilege was being challenged.

I envisioned all kinds of negative responses from readers, but when the article appeared that Sunday in December, nothing happened. No angry phone calls, no one marched in front of my house, nothing. I was initially relieved, then disappointed. I did get some affirming statements from friends.

I come by my nervousness honestly. I was not accustomed to putting my opinions out there. I spent most of my professional life purposefully not expressing public opinions about political, social, or religious issues. As a psychotherapist, I thought it important that any client who came through my door not have preconceived ideas about my politics or my religious background. Clients come in with plenty of baggage already about therapy and therapists. I didn't want to add to the mix. In addition, as a psychologist at a state university, I had lived with some restrictions about making personal views public on such topics, lest I be seen as promoting the university's viewpoint.

Upon retirement, I wanted to write more. I had written plenty in my work, but that writing took the form of manuals, presentations, case notes, brochures, and other documents necessary for the functioning of a large counseling center. I decided on opinion articles for the newspaper as one of my venues. Once I overcame the initial nerves, I realized that either not that many people read them or not that many felt inclined to respond, though I have been called a few unflattering names in on-line comments.

My purpose in writing opinion articles is less about expressing my own opinions, and more about widening the discussion. Political, social, and religious issues are too often discussed in the simplest possible terms, usually with a predetermined judgment in mind. Most of us go about looking for information and opinions that coincide with what we already believe. When it comes to issues that affect us personally, we rarely listen or read in order to gather new information that may broaden our perspective. We're not looking for change. We're looking for confirmation.

Writing these articles has prompted me to get beyond finding only what I'm looking for. Writing is a discovery activity. If I don't learn something from the preparation or the writing, I doubt anyone will learn from what I produce. As I read through these articles for inclusion in this book, I discovered some recurring themes; so recurring, in fact, I worried that I was just saying the same thing over and over. What I discovered was that I was expressing many of the same values in response to different events.

The articles are divided into four categories. These categories overlap, but they provide a way to organize and present the articles. The categories are:
- Words matter
- Family, loss, and life's uncertainties
- Inclusiveness and diversity
- The uneasy alliance of Christianity and politics

Reviewing these articles has reminded me that I have changed. Writing them has helped me put up some landmarks to show where I am now, to help me look back to where I came from, and to give me reference for where I'm headed.

TABLE OF CONTENTS

WORDS MATTER

Political and social concerns are complex, too complex for any of us to have a full understanding or appreciation of their implications. Because discussion and understanding should be our goal for issues that impact our lives, it becomes necessary to simplify those issues enough to allow discussion to take place.

However, oversimplification leaves out crucial context and differing perspectives, turning a complex matter into a false dichotomy, a yes/no proposition. "This situation can impact your life in a thousand ways no one can fully predict. Are you for or against it?" That's a false dichotomy. When this happens, discussion and discovery stop and people take sides.

Another popular strategy for putting an end to discussion and discovery is to divert attention away from the issue and instead focus on the person making the argument. By name-calling or labeling someone with a derogatory term, the complex issue at hand gets lost.

Words are our most powerful tools. The following essays address ways we can use words for clarification and understanding or for blustering, confusing, and demeaning.

ARGUMENTUM AD HOMINEM
July 14, 2018

"Canada does not believe that *ad hominem* attacks are a
particularly appropriate or useful way to conduct our
relations with other countries."

***

CHRYSTIA FREELAND, CANADIAN FOREIGN AFFAIRS MINISTER

Huh? This was the Canadian response to President Trump's
advisers following their criticism of the Prime Minister after the
G7 meetings. The response was clear and direct, yet subtle and
reasonable. Trump and his advisors got taken to school and to the
woodshed at the same time.

I had to look up *ad hominem*. I'd heard the phrase before and had a
vague idea of what it meant, but to hear it used both casually and
precisely prompted an immediate search.

Ad hominem is short for *argumentum ad hominem* (Latin). This is
an argumentative strategy in which the genuine topic at hand is
avoided by instead attacking the character, motive, or other attribute
of the person making the argument. In other words, if you are thin
on information, discredit your opponent. Take attention away from
the fact that you have no bullets in your mental clip and instead, call

2

your opponent derogatory names or make stuff up about the one who is showing you up.

Our president is a master of this strategy. Like a child with a mallet as his only toy, everything gets pounded. This is his default approach when responding to disagreement. Beginning with his campaign, he gave each of the Republican candidates a denigrating nickname. Whenever the debates ranged into an area in which he could not hold his own, which included almost every topic, he used the nicknames and turned a debate about issues into an attack on the person.

Our president did not invent this strategy, nor is he the first to use it in political discourse. However, he has elevated it to a dangerous level, using it now in global diplomacy, and practicing it so often in daily utterances that he has normalized the strategy. We are no longer appalled when he belittles, and we're no longer surprised when no one confronts him on this unpresidential, adolescent behavior.

With a Supreme Court nomination and mid-term elections approaching, we can expect a new barrage of this approach from both sides.

But this is not just about the president. I too am guilty. I rarely discuss politics with anyone who may have a different opinion, because I too often end up walking away muttering "What an idiot" rather than having a conversation. *Argumentum ad hominem* at work.

These days, separating the issue from the person is difficult. That, to me, is behind much of the polarization in our nation. For one example, when a football player takes a knee during the national anthem, the player is attacked as unpatriotic and the discussion about the treatment of people of color in our country is derailed. *Argumentum ad hominem* at work.

Bring up any issue; reproductive choice, gun regulation, immigration, same-sex rights, voter suppression, health care; then watch for the labeling and nicknaming that ensues, each label bearing baggage that may or may not be true for the person stating the opinion.

These and a host of other issues are not merely problems to be solved. These are complex and multi-faceted realities that need to be addressed with attention to the consequences to all who are impacted by those realities.

We have a president who has shown little propensity to consider complexity or consequence. Instead, he simplifies these life-altering issues into win-lose events, encouraging people to line up on his side or the other. Regardless of the passion involved, such issues are NEVER simple. NEVER.

I make an issue seem simple when I see it only through my own eyes and how it will impact me. Then it's easy to come down on one side or the other and assign labels to everyone else. Simplification makes name-calling easier, almost necessary. *Argumentum ad hominem* at work.

That gets me nowhere. I have to start by listening, really listening with genuine curiosity, without an agenda, without trying to persuade the other, without trying to win. That's hard. It's nearly impossible in today's politics. These days I rarely listen with ears and heart wide open. I rarely listen in order to learn what makes the other person tick, what brought them to the conclusion that differs from mine, what scares and motivates them to hold the positions they hold. That's where I have to start. It's just so much easier to walk away muttering, "What an idiot."

Argumentum ad hominem at work.

STICKS AND STONES
March 3, 2019

The old adage, "Sticks and stones may break my bones, but words will never hurt me," has never been true. Words are powerful and have the potential to hurt, to comfort, to enrage, to heal. A few weeks ago in an opinion article in this newspaper, the author lamented the loss of toughness in our society today, suggesting that people who allowed words to have an adverse effect on them were thin-skinned. He was referring to bullying and to statements used to disparage a person or a group.

The author described the people who got offended as being touchy-feely, overly sensitive, thinking that any negative statement is "a crime worse than murder," causing them to want "to commit suicide or call the SWAT team." I hope he was being hyperbolic, not literal.

Does he not realize that remarks that are racist, homophobic, sexist, that in any way belittle or disparage an individual or group have a corrosive effect? Even casual remarks that may go unnoticed by those outside the targeted group can do damage.

The author of the article is a member of all the same majority groups of which I am a member; white, male, middle class, middle aged (or older), heterosexual, Christian. These designations allow us the privilege of distance, distance from understanding the sting of such statements, and distance enough to criticize those who make such statements as well as those who are hurt by them. However, our challenge as the privileged majority is to not stand at a distance and shake our heads, but instead to also be offended by hurtful statements aimed at others.

The author suggests that kids should not allow bullying and other forms of harassment to bother them. That's an adult perspective. Adults have, or at least should have, the life experience, self-awareness, and emotional maturity to allow senseless statements to go by without impact. Children and adolescents, however, often do not yet have the life history or emotional maturity to evaluate and then dismiss offensive statements. It's not just about self-esteem, as the author suggests. It is also a matter of social and emotional development.

Bullying IS a problem for today's youth. Not just the physical intimidation I experienced as a kid, but also the verbal bullying and cyber-bullying that, because of social media, can spread embarrassment and shame to a kid's entire social network in a matter of seconds. That is the stuff of adolescent suicide. As an adult, I can only imagine the helplessness of having a shameful lie circulated to my entire personal and vocational network without any way for me to stop or mitigate the damage. Sticks and stones would be a welcome alternative.

As a society, we must go far beyond being nice and kind. Contrary to the author's perspective, we no longer live in a society that teaches us to be polite. Our culture is becoming increasingly hostile, even violent. Just look at the political hostility and name-calling that we now treat as normal. This may seem normal, but it is not good.

We must go beyond being nice. We must move to respect and to awareness of the impact we have on one another.

We can no longer claim ignorance of the issue. Words have power and we must take responsibility for our words. Listen to most apologies by public figures. The common apology is, "I'm sorry if anyone was offended by my words." This statement suggests, "I didn't say anything wrong, but some people chose to be offended." The only thing missing from the apology is, "Shame on you all for being so sensitive."

I want to hear a public figure say, "I'm sorry, I said an offensive thing. I didn't realize what I said was offensive. I obviously have some things to learn."

As a psychologist, I worked with many women and men who grew up in physically and sexually abusive families. I worked with people who identified as LGBTQ who had been disowned by family and church. I worked with people of color who grew up surrounded by subtle and overt racism. In our work together, we didn't have to scratch very far below the surface before finding intense pain and rage. Were they "overly sensitive" to unkind remarks? Absolutely, and for good reason.

Instead of criticizing people for being thin-skinned or overly sensitive, how about we focus on the intent of those who say disparaging things, confront them, and then support those who are hurt.

RESPECTFUL CURIOSITY
January 5, 2008

A few years back in my work as a psychotherapist, I met with a young woman who had requested to work with a Christian counselor, so I wasn't surprised when one of her first questions was, "Are you a Christian?"

I responded, "If I tell you I am a Christian, you will assume some things about me that are not true. If I tell you I am not a Christian, you will assume other things about me that are not true." I then asked her to tell me what it was about having a Christian counselor that was important to her. Her response began a very productive therapy relationship, but we first had to clarify what the label "Christian" meant to her.

Labels are necessary. They are mental, verbal, and social shortcuts. Without them we'd spend all our time explaining every little thing about ourselves in order to get to know one another. Therefore, we use career labels such as accountant, beautician, pharmacist, or rancher. We use political labels, Republican, liberal, and socialist. We use labels to identify race, culture, religion; you get the idea. Each label comes with some efficient, built-in assumptions. But that's where their use becomes problematic.

Labels can reduce a person or a group to a single characteristic or simplistic identity. When I moved from Austin to Central Illinois many years ago, I was warned I'd be living among "northerners and Yankees." Instead I found a lot of people who became valued colleagues and dear friends, as well as some folks I didn't care for. The relationships I developed had very little to do with my initial assumptions of "northerners." Fortunately I did not live down to many of their unkind assumptions about "southerners and Texans."

Even worse than simplifying, we can degrade or dismiss a person or a group with a single word or phrase. Notice the efficient savagery of labels during this political campaign. Complex, intelligent, committed people running in both parties are reduced to unprincipled morons. Once certain labels are introduced, particularly with the appropriate sneer, we no longer debate the substance of the issue, nor do we see the person. Instead, we take sides around the label and productive discussion grinds to a halt.

It's one thing to label people based on choices they've made, words they've spoken, or actions they've taken. It's quite another thing to label and judge someone based on who they are by nature. I didn't choose to be Caucasian. I didn't decide to be male or blue-eyed or heterosexual or left-handed. I didn't choose the family or culture into which I was born. For someone to sneer at me for being a left-handed, blue-eyed heterosexual is ludicrous. Yet racism, sexism, heterosexism, and other social abuses are based on just such notions. In this political season and in our lives in general, we could all benefit from what a friend of mine calls "respectful curiosity." Beginning with respectful curiosity leaves room to discover something more about the person or the group we don't understand.

When I am respectfully curious, I often discover that the person whose life on the surface looks radically different from mine is usually dealing as well as they can with most of the same kinds of concerns I am dealing with. It's hard to be respectfully curious and self-righteous at the same time.

POLITICAL CORRECTNESS
December 13, 2015

"Political correctness" is getting a bad name. Throughout this presidential campaign, Donald Trump has insisted that political correctness was killing our country. Candidates generally choose their words carefully, but now, if they are too careful, they can be accused of being PC and contributing to our country's demise. This has allowed some, namely Donald Trump, to say whatever comes to mind, regardless of how hurtful, disrespectful, or unconstitutional it might be. At least they're not being PC.

"Political correctness" seems different today than a couple of decades ago. In the 1980s and '90s, political correctness focused more on helping those of us in the majority to recognize and correct our cultural blindness. Men needed to become more aware of how we minimized women with language. Whites had to recognize the damage our language perpetuated on people of color. Heterosexuals had to wise up about how our depictions of gays and lesbians were not only insensitive, but also harmful.

The purpose of being called out for being politically incorrect was to provide teachable moments to those of us in the majority. Our casual and usually thoughtless language kept hurtful and harmful beliefs entrenched, thus perpetuating the cultural divide that minority groups saw clearly while those of us in the majority remained blind. It was not about anyone or any group being thin-skinned or picky, it was about getting through the thick skulls of those of us in the majority.

The current focus on political correctness is quite different. We have moved from finding teachable moments to looking for "gotcha" moments. Teachable moments prompt discussion. Gotcha moments shut it down.

In a discussion of cultural differences several years ago, one of my colleagues, a Hispanic woman, confronted me on something I said. She was not accusatory, just observant. "Did you know that you said...?" I didn't realize it. I was embarrassed. I got defensive. She responded simply, "I just need you to know what effect that has on me."

I finally responded, "I've said that all my life without thinking about it. I had no idea it was offensive to anyone. I'm sorry." That was it. She had been heard, I had learned, the discussion moved on.

That doesn't seem to happen much these days. There is little room to disagree and then continue to talk. When it comes to the hot topics of today, such as terrorism, gun regulation, abortion, immigration, same-sex marriage, climate change, disagreement rarely produces discussion. Instead, disagreement generally leads to each side trying to outshout the other with the assumption, "I'm right and you're an idiot." No one hears or learns anything new.

In politics, candidates are criticized for being too cautious. Ironically, on college campuses, professors must now be wary of not being cautious enough. Students and professors who introduce or discuss topics that might be upsetting to students run the risk of having a grievance or lawsuit filed against them. In a setting where the exchange of divergent ideas should be encouraged, there is little room for navigating between being honest and being seen as oppressive.

Political correctness does not have to be a sign of weakness or cowardice. Being careful not to offend a group of people is a sign that we are at least talking about something that is uncomfortable and important, and probably at one time unmentionable. Finding appropriate words with the intention of not offending someone is a huge step.

Being honest and genuine, speaking my mind while still being respectful and compassionate is a tough balance that requires a level of humility and openness I am generally not willing to invest. I have to ask myself if I am just as willing to listen and learn as I am to speak and be heard. If so, I then have to keep my mouth shut and listen. I have to be genuinely curious about the other's perspective. "Tell me more about…" "How did you come to that opinion?" Only then can I expect them to take me seriously.

Words are important. They are our best tools for creating a world where we can all live together. The path toward compassion and respect usually begins with ignorance. The path then passes through patches of awkward, politically incorrect statements and misunderstandings. If we stay with it, we find the words we need and the respect others deserve so we can continue down the path.

IN PRAISE OF THE BEER SUMMIT
August 9, 2009

On July 30, 2009, President Obama hosted the event that became known as "The Beer Summit" in response to a situation that had sparked a national debate.

Harvard University professor Henry Louis Gates Jr. was returning home to Cambridge after a trip to China. Gates found the front door to his home jammed shut and, with the help of his driver, tried to force it open. A local witness reported their activity to the police as a potential burglary in progress. Local police officer, Sgt. James Crowley, arrived, a confrontation ensued, and Gates was arrested and charged with disorderly conduct. The charges against Gates were dropped, but the arrest generated a national debate about what appeared to be racial profiling by police.

The President invited Gates, Crowley, and Vice President Joe Biden to the White House to sit down in a courtyard near the Rose Garden, have a beer, and talk about what had happened.

I find it amusing that so many people found so many things to criticize about the recent "beer summit." I loved it. A refreshing response to a volatile situation. The media whined, "If this is such a teachable moment, why won't they let us be there to record what they are saying?" The media didn't get it. The teachable moment was not about what the participants said to each other over beer. The teachable moment came when four people, each embroiled in a conflict, sat down in a relaxed setting to talk. What a novel idea.

Such an approach seems far too civil to be taken seriously. Most of what passes for political and social discourse these days takes a far different course. On TV, on the floors of congress, and on the radio talk shows, we typically get opinionated "experts" who are given microphones and then encouraged to go after each other. Each assumes that the other is uninformed, morally inferior, or simply a moron. The advantage goes not to the one with the best argument or the most accurate information, but to the one who can talk louder, faster, and can more effectively talk over everyone else, including the moderator. Lots of smoke, very little fire.

Each works to redefine and simplify the issue so that one opinion becomes truth and every other opinion is simply wrong. It's OK to attack the personal arguments, but if that's not enough, it's standard practice to attack personal character as well. It's a verbal prizefight where points are given for the most low blows landed.

Is anything accomplished with such an approach? Our opinions about the issues don't change. We, the listeners, almost always end up holding onto the opinion we had in the beginning and disagreeing even more stridently with the opposing view. We see and hear precisely what we expect to see and hear. Nothing new happens, ever.

Unlike such "debates," dialogue is collaborative. Whether it's over beer in the White House rose garden, over coffee in the diner, or over lunch with a colleague, the object of a dialogue is not to "win" but to more fully understand one another, both the differences and the commonalities. Imagine groups of African Americans and Anglos, Christians and Muslims, straights and gays, or any other group that has a history of misunderstanding, sitting down for a dialogue.

What if we gave ourselves time to really listen, to allow both sides to expand on the issues, to recognize that things are not as simple and clear-cut as we'd like to believe. Wouldn't it be interesting if each person in such a dialogue realized that he or she did not possess some ultimate truth, but that personal truths have been shaped, bent, and limited by personal experience. Maybe we would have a little more space for learning about the other's perspective if we exhibited the same openness we want from them.

What a thought: opposing sides gaining respect for each other rather than trying to score a knockout. Dialogue does not assume we will all agree, but out of dialogue can come creative options we could never think of while we're busy yelling and not listening.

I don't know what transpired as Crowley, Gates, Obama, and Biden sat sipping and snacking. The fact that they sat down together, they talked, they shared food and drink, and then they went their separate ways peacefully is enough. Each reported a greater appreciation for the part each of them played in the racial drama. That speaks volumes, far more than a transcript of their conversation.

And so, Mr. President, for understanding that dialogue can be a tool for change, and for demonstrating that understanding can sometimes accomplish what coercion can't, this Bud's for you.

TEACHABLE MOMENTS
September 29, 2018

A teachable moment is an unplanned, fleeting opportunity in which circumstance and readiness come together in a single experience. Such a moment provides a timely opportunity for a new insight to emerge. Effective teachers and parents recognize them. So do effective bosses and supervisors.

These moments of insight and growth rarely present themselves when all is going well. In those moments we are in no hurry to change anything. Teachable moments more often come in the midst of confusion, conflict, loss, disappointment, or painfully discovering our limits. Whenever we feel vulnerable, confused, or lost, we are ripe for something unexpected.

The classroom is not the only place for a teachable moment. They happen at home, at work, among friends, and on a national level.

We as a nation have seen many teachable moments come and go in the past months. Colin Kaepernick provided one such moment. Regardless of your position on his action, it is clear that people of good faith, true patriotism, and a strong desire for justice have come down on both sides. The "Me, too" and "Time's up" movements, as well as the current Supreme Court confirmation hearings of Brett Kavanaugh, have given us many opportunities to broaden our understanding of and response to sexual assault. Every school shooting has provided fertile ground for genuine discussions about common sense responses to gun violence. Those are just a few of the many social and political issues that have the potential to be teachable moments for our nation.

One hallmark of effective leadership is the ability to identify and seize upon such moments. To do so, the leader must recognize that the issues and the conflicts that follow are always more complex than they appear, that the "Why?" question never has an easy answer. Teachable moments show up when we recognize that we don't understand the complexity and we don't have a simple "why." At that point we are ready for something new.

Sadly, our president has consistently chosen to ignore teachable moments. He seems unaware of nuance and complexity. His approach is to simplify the issue, to make disparaging statements about those who disagree with him, and to encourage his followers to take his side. He has chosen division by making every issue a forced choice, an "us against them" situation.

Effective leaders understand that when people have conflicts, it is because they value different things or they fear different things, not simply because one side is right and the other is wrong. Again, our president seems unaware of this reality.

In every conflict the leader has at least two options. One option is to bring conflicted parties together, not to force an agreement, but to talk, listen, and provide the possibility of seeing the conflict more broadly. This may produce a resolution that suits both sides. It may not. At least it creates greater understanding and will likely reveal that the two opposing sides have some areas of agreement they didn't recognize. That's a teachable moment.

The other option is to divide by simplifying and moralizing the issue, thus allowing those in conflict to get more entrenched in their own views and more opposed to the other views. This is the approach most often used by our president, though it is not exclusive to the president. As a nation we've never been very good at managing disagreements. These days, though, the impulse to divide rather than communicate, the approach espoused by our president, has trickled down into all levels of government and into our social structures so that it is starting to feel normal, even inevitable.

As a parent, I had to learn and relearn the concept of teachable moments. No matter how eloquent my lectures, no matter how reasonable or intense my arguments, regardless of how much I whined, complained, scolded, encouraged, or guilted, if my children were not open and ready to hear from me, I was powerless. Readiness came when things fell apart for one of them. If I was willing to be the adult in the room when they were ready, something good almost always happened.

We are an adolescent nation. We have been fortunate to have many leaders who could be the adult in the room and help us through teachable moments. In the absence of such a leader now, and with a congress and Supreme Court so polarized and politicized, we as a nation are left in a precarious situation.

SCHISMS CAUSED BY FEAR
February 16, 2014

Talking with a local pastor over coffee this past week, he lamented about a growing schism in his denomination in which large numbers of conservatives were leaving the denomination. He didn't go into detail, but I suspect that the issue behind the conflict was the inclusion and ordination of gays and lesbians.

I commented to the pastor that schisms such as this appear to be not only a denominational concern, but also a cultural, national, even global phenomenon. Consider, for example, the gridlock in Washington over almost anything, the intensity of feelings locally and globally around a host of hot-button issues such as abortion or marriage equality, the incessant vitriol aimed at our president as well as at his detractors, and the rise of radical fundamentalism in the Christian and Muslim world, just to name a few.

Ideological differences today no longer seem to prompt debate. More often they prompt labeling and moralizing. When that happens, we simply entrench ourselves and fortify our position. Differences become reasons for divisions rather than opportunities for discussion and learning.

A news commentator said recently, "Financial uncertainty creates moral crisis." That is, when we perceive that something dear to us is falling apart, we want to find someone to blame for the situation. When things feel shaky, it is human nature to try to nail things down, to impose certainty wherever we can in order to establish an illusion of control, comfort, and safety.

One of our methods of imposing certainty is to label something or someone as good or bad, right or wrong, decent or indecent. Once labeled, we have one thing we have nailed down, and we can feel good about aligning ourselves with the people and issues that fit our criteria.

This labeling and moralizing pertains to events as well. This past week, when my daughter called to say she just lost her job, my first reaction was, "Oh no, that's terrible!" I used more colorful language, but that was the sentiment. After some reflection though, I remembered that some such "Oh no!" events in my life turned out to be some of my best opportunities for learning, growth, and new opportunities. I didn't and still don't have the wisdom to know if something is good or bad because I have no idea how the situation will ultimately turn out.

When I overheard an acquaintance say a few days ago, "Our society has been in free fall for quite some time," I thought, one person's "free fall" is likely another person's "finally, the right direction!" We see from our own perspective and we're simply not wise enough to know how it will turn out.

These ideological divisions are not new, but a new level of paranoia and hostility seems to be at work. Today anyone, from a bullied teenager to a billionaire financing a Super PAC, can spin or even invent a story, send it around the world instantly on-line, and then sit back and enjoy the reactions without experiencing any personal consequences. That reality alone makes the situation today potentially more volatile.

That fact places a greater responsibility on each of us to question the source and challenge the motivation of the many divisive statements we hear. If we don't, we contribute to the hostility and miss a chance to learn something.

As a grief counselor, I recognized how important it was for the grieving person to fall apart occasionally. Life is like that. It comes together, it falls apart, it comes back together, and falls apart again. Our task is not to nail everything down. Our task is to be as fully aware of the falling apart as we are of the coming together. Both phases of the process possess vital lessons for living.

Back to the denominational schism. The Apostle Paul wrote regarding divisions in the early church, "...there is neither Jew nor Greek, slave or free, male or female." Those were the hot topics of his day, the things people fought about. Today I suspect he would write, "...there is neither Black nor White, gay nor straight, liberal nor conservative..."

What a thought.

SIMPLIFICATION IS NOT THE SOLUTION
November 10, 2014

"The cause of the draught in the Southwest is a lack of rainfall." A friend read this newspaper quote to me as we sat together over coffee. I'm sure that the climate expert being quoted had much more than that to say about draught, but the stand-alone sentence left us both speechless. This became a hilarious theme of our subsequent conversations that morning. "The cause of the team's losing record is a lack of points." "The cause of the person's death was a lack of heart beats." You get the idea. The sentence was so preposterous in its simplicity, it begged to be played with.

The sentence provides a great example of how we so often think simplistically about issues that are in fact complex. This particular sentence was taken from an article about climate change, an issue of such scientific complexity that some simplification is needed if we nonclimatologists are to understand and converse about it. But too often we overly simplify other issues, particularly social, moral, ethical, and political ones that should be addressed in their complexity.

Recent examples abound. During last month's government shutdown and debt-ceiling debate, each side slanted and simplified issues of enormous complexity and consequence, because doing so allowed them to then stand at a microphone and accuse the other side of not negotiating on issues that, from their perspective, were simple and clear.

Similarly, we simplify the debate over abortion into two hyphenated phrases: Pro-Life and Pro-Choice. Once framed into team names, we can choose sides without really thinking through the emotional, medical, moral, and social complexities. Once we've chosen our team, we can assume that we have the moral high ground and can then label the others as immoral or uncaring or worse.

The diverse views about the Second Amendment are boiled down into one phrase, "gun control." The use of the word "control" is enough to drive people into camps of "for" and "against" where they can cheer their cause without acknowledging the wide variety of common-sense options available to protect public safety as well as insure constitutional rights. It's not surprising that both sides of the debate use recent acts of violence to promote their own narrow perspective.

It seems that whatever issue is being debated in Austin or in Washington, simplification and polarization are the goals, gridlock the result. The Affordable Care Act, immigration reform, marriage equality, climate change, education reform, the buying and selling of political influence, and a host of other issues get simplified to the point that no useful discussion in public or on the congressional floor takes place.

If any of these issues were really that simple, solutions would be simple, even obvious. The fact that the views are so diverse and so passionate should be a clue that, rather than immediately taking sides, we need to ask, "What more do I need to know?" Too often, though, most of us, I include myself, ask only one question, "How will this affect me?" Once that question becomes the focus, we settle for the answers that support our predetermined position and our own personal interests.

Whenever a complex issue is summarized into a bumper sticker slogan, and whenever we are encouraged to think only of our own situation, information becomes irrelevant and critical thinking is unnecessary.

If our leaders are simply making proclamations from entrenched partisan positions rather than researching, collaborating, seeking solutions, and voting their conscience, they are not doing their jobs.

If we as the voting public are simply listening to those with whom we already agree, if we are simply hunkering down and defending our position against all arguments, regardless of fact, reason, or consequence, we are not doing our jobs.

HOSTILITY OR CIVILITY?
January 16. 2011

U.S. Representative Gabrielle Giffords and eighteen others were shot on January 8, 2011 during a constituent meeting called "Congress on Your Corner," held in a Safeway parking lot in Casas Adobes, Arizona. Six of those who were shot died.

In the wake of the Tucson shootings, a recurring theme in the news has been the need to tone down the hostile rhetoric in politics and in society in general. The Pima County Sheriff sounded the alarm first when he cited the "vitriol" in our society as being a contributing factor to such acts of violence. His words hit a chord, there was a collective nod of agreement, and then the finger-pointing began, trying to identify who's responsible for all the hostility. And of course, the blaming and the defending grew increasingly hostile.

My goal in writing this article was to support this call for greater respect and civility in our society and to address the damage that words can do on a personal and societal level. As I wrote, something interesting happened within me. As I cited examples of people and groups that I thought were contributing to the problem, my words got antagonistic and blaming, and my tone became self-righteous. I took a deep breath and started over, this time trying to be more circumspect. Within a few sentences, the same thing happened. I grew hostile writing about hostility!

So how am I supposed to respond? After all, my first response to hostility toward me or toward a person or cause I support is to become defensive, which easily turns into retaliation. As much as I see myself as a conciliatory person, I can generate some pretty mean thoughts with just a tiny spark of provocation.

President Obama, in his speech in Tucson, said, "We are far too eager to lay the blame at the feet of those who happen to think differently than we do." I'm pretty sure he nodded at me when he said that. It's much easier for all of us to focus on the causes or on those we believe are responsible for all the hostility. It's much more difficult to simply do my part to stop the cycle of hostility, regardless of who started it, particularly when my part includes not retaliating.

So again, how am I to respond when my neck hairs are standing up? I have learned that I first have to breathe and remember a few things. I have to remember that hostility, my own or someone else's, is always based in fear. All the red-faced yelling and stomping and posturing are about feeling threatened. If I respond in kind with my own fearful anger, there is never a resolution. Hostility simply reinforces hostility because it confirms our fears.

Some of my hostile therapy clients taught me a thing or two. One said loudly, "This isn't helping. You don't know what the hell you're doing." If I had responded with a defensive, "Oh yes I do," or with a self-righteous, "Hey, I'm just trying to help," his fears about the process and his doubts about me would have been confirmed. If, on the other hand, I manage to keep my wits and respond to his fear with respectful curiosity, such as, "You're right, this hasn't been easy for either of us. There's a lot about you I don't understand yet. Are you willing to stick with me a little longer?" we might get somewhere. I must somehow disengage from the hostility. Otherwise I get caught in it. "Disengage" doesn't mean I ignore or deny the fear and the anger. It means I see it for what it is and choose instead to engage with the person with respect, curiosity, and openness to what they have to say.

Even as I write these words, I'm saying to myself, "Good idea, John, but can you really do that?" Hostility seems so built-in to our national discourse these days. Of course we can do something, but we must give up the idea that we have to be right and that others therefore have to be wrong. We must embrace the idea that we each have something to learn from the other, even the other who is so different we get scared. It also requires that we keep our mouth shut until we have heard the other person fully and clearly. I'd rather jump in as soon as I have formulated a rebuttal. That's the hard part. It's far easier just to blame.

VICTIMS NEED TO BE HEARD
April 7, 2018

Now that we have heard from the children, will we be the adults?

I was impressed, humbled, and inspired by the teenagers who participated in the March for Our Lives. The speakers stood in front of hundreds of thousands of marchers, knowing also that millions more were watching them on television, and still they spoke with poise, passion, and focus. Far more than I had at that age.

I believe they deserve our admiration and our attention, and they deserve to be taken seriously. But what would it mean to take them seriously? A few weeks ago in an editorial, Jonah Goldberg objected to the "fetishization of youth in politics" and warned against "celebrating young people as inherently wiser and more moral that adults."

His objections are based on a false premise. Most people know that youth are not inherently wiser or more moral than adults. Their views will evolve and change with experience, just as ours have and will. Some of their opinions and views will mellow with time, others will deepen and intensify. But we must not ignore their wisdom or their moral focus now. They have been traumatized by a great evil and they mustered the courage to speak and act rather than retreat.

The reason we should listen to them is that they are the primary stakeholders in the issue of gun violence in schools and on the streets. They are the ones getting shot. These students in particular have had an assault rifle aimed in their direction. They are the ones who hid in closets and heard the rounds being fired, not knowing when the shooter would find them. They deserve our attention and our respect, even if we don't agree with them. Even if we think they are immature.

In the discussions about common-sense gun legislation, the students and teachers are the ones who will live or die by the outcome. They have literal skin in the game and they deserve to be listened to.

The primary stakeholders should always have a voice. Not just in gun legislation, but it all issues. Any time the decisions of the powerful affect the lives of the more vulnerable, the voices of those affected need to be heard and heeded.

For example, I was dismayed at the photo a year ago of a conference room in the White House in which 30 white men were sitting around a conference table discussing women's health care. In a room where people are making proposals and decisions about women's health care, the only men present should be those serving coffee.

In Texas, retired teachers are discovering the financially devastating impact of our state legislators' decisions about health care. Those legislators eased the burden of their own health care costs while passing a crippling burden on to others who have spent a career educating children. The teachers are the stakeholders. The legislators should not be the beneficiaries.

Our leaders, sitting in positions of power and privilege, make decisions about health care, the social safety net, education, and other enormous issues that affect people who have little access to that power. In every social or political decision, how would things be different if those most affected by the decision were given not just a voice, but were included in the decision-making?

This is consistent with the Biblical admonition to attend to the needs of the least of these, those most vulnerable and most disadvantaged by the power system. The Bible singles out the widows and orphans, those who are hungry and sick, those in prison. Those were the neediest of that day. They had no safety net, no recourse. Today, in our diverse society, the list of the vulnerable is long. The list includes people of color, women, the hungry and homeless, the sick without health care coverage, just for starters.

The question for our culture is, "Are we willing to chip away some of our rights and privileges in order to address a greater need of someone more vulnerable?"

Should we do exactly what those teenagers want done? Of course not. I rolled my eyes when they demanded their needs be addressed "Right now." That's the passion of youth. But we should not dismiss their substance simply because we don't feel their passion. Goldberg correctly stated that young people have a gift for cutting through the false pieties and polite fictions of modern life.

Getting shot at will do that, I guess. The stakeholders, regardless of the issue, deserve to be taken seriously.

FAMILY/LOSS/LIFE'S UNCERTAINTIES

I don't learn much when things are going well. At those times I want to enjoy the cruise, not rock the boat. I learn my most important lessons when things fall apart. That's when life gets my attention. Once I get beyond dreading what's coming next or feeling sorry for myself, I can eventually get to the place of paying attention and asking, "What do I need to learn from this?"

No better classrooms exist for life's lessons than one's family, moments of significant loss, and encountering life's uncertainties. These shaping influences are always with us. We never fully move beyond our family's gravitational pull. As we grow and change, we grieve the loss of what was once familiar, even necessary. And of course, life's uncertainties are all around us all the time. Much of the time we can ignore these shaping influences, but better to see them and let them teach us as they present themselves.

JUST ENOUGH LIGHT
February 10, 2008

As kids, my brothers and I craned our necks, trying to see beyond the next curve in the winding dirt road that was barely wide enough for our dad to maneuver the car between giant pines.

A canopy of limbs and leaves overhead added to the anticipation as we bumped along toward the cottage. The rustic, wood-frame house nestled in the midst of a patch of woods in southern Maine was my favorite vacation spot as a youngster. Years later, it became the favorite vacation spot for my kids.

There are many things to love about the place—walking in the woods, sitting by the water, lounging in front of the fireplace, exploring the cluttered corners of the upstairs sleeping loft. What makes all this even more intriguing is that the cottage has no electricity. There are no switches on the wall, no lights in the ceiling, nowhere to plug things in. As the sun goes down, kerosene lanterns provide the light.

Using lanterns takes some getting used to. A lantern doesn't light up the whole place. It gives a faint glow to the room, but most of the light is righter there close to the flame. The light is fine for reading, but if I want to go into the kitchen for snack, I have to take a lantern with me. Otherwise, I'll be fumbling around in the dark.

The light moves with me as I carry it, and there is just enough light for the task at hand. Lanterns require a bit more mindfulness and patience. But this only adds to the mystery and excitement of the whole experience, because when the sun goes down, it gets dark. Really dark.

As a psychologist on a college campus, I encountered many students who expected their university experience to be a process of turning on lights. Many hoped their academic learning would be a process of flipping switches, progressively making everything clear and understandable. Others expected their experience to be like a beacon that would shine far down the career path, illuminating their future plans and the outcomes to their present decisions. The fact is that the college experience more often resembles a lantern. So does life in general.

I am wary of people who speak with false certainty, who claim to have some kind of divine beacon or floodlight of wisdom. Political figures that smugly make guarantees about providing national safety, economic well-being, or anything for that matter don't give me much confidence.

I run from those who proclaim religion as fact over faith or who preach about the certainty rather than the mystery of things spiritual. I am skeptical of anyone who wants me to adopt their version of how things are, as if they have the inside track on truth. Most of these folks are using either fear or promises of prosperity to promote their brand of certainty. But if you scratch the surface of such certainty, you'll find a person promoting self rather than proclaiming truth.

Life is uncertain. We have always lived in uncertain times. We are simply more aware of it these days. Life is always changing, and we either learn from life or we retreat in fear or false certainty. Decision-making is always our best guess at the time, based on our present information or lack of information. Each of us has only a lantern.

The Psalmist who said, "Your word is a lamp unto my feet, a light to my path," was speaking of a tiny oil lamp that gave just enough light for the next step and dispelled just enough darkness to take that step. A lantern is all we have. But when it's dark, really dark, a lantern will do just fine.

CRISIS IN FAITH
April 26, 2009

I attended "Youth Sunday" at church a few weeks ago. I'm always a bit unnerved watching teenagers lead worship. I sympathize with those who struggle with the public presentation part. I sympathize even more with those trying to articulate their faith at that time in their lives. These are flashback to my youth ministry days, I suppose, when I felt some responsibility for their public as well as their personal preparation.

As a university psychotherapist and professor, I talked with numerous students over the years who stated in a variety of ways, "I am losing my faith," or "I no longer believe in God."

I wanted to say, "Congratulations!" because I saw this as a moment of great potential. However, no one wants to hear that in the midst of distress. The truth was, most were not losing their faith. They were finding that their childhood faith no longer fit their young adult life. The beliefs that had gotten them through childhood and high school were no longer able to provide guidance for their expanding world and growing challenges. They were losing their outdated faith and developing a more mature understanding of God, themselves, and their place in the world.

Such a crisis in faith, however, does not usually feel like positive growth. It is more often frightening and disorienting. It feels like a loss, a crisis of identity, an abandonment of the past, a shaking of life's foundation. Nonetheless, it's an important, even necessary process.

Entomology of all things provides a useful picture of what's happening. Insects have a hard exoskeleton rather than an inner skeleton. The exoskeleton provides protection and support, but because it is rigid, it does not expand as the insect grows. Periodically, usually after hibernation, the insect must shed its outer shell to make way for the new growth.

The first step in this process is to produce a new exoskeleton under the old one. The new one is soft and pliable. The insect's body then secretes enzymes that begin dissolving the old exoskeleton. The shell eventually splits, and the insect works its way out. All those cicada husks on tree trunks in the spring show the result of this process.

Just after molting, the insect is most vulnerable to predators because the new shell has not yet fully formed and hardened. Until the exoskeleton fully develops, the insect has difficulty moving and it lacks the protection provided by the exoskeleton.

A crisis in faith feels like losing the exoskeleton. Even though it no longer fit, it provided some structure and protection.

Inner change takes place during important transitions associated with growth. For example, when I went away to college, my life changed. I encountered people who had beliefs and ideas far different from mine. These new ideas and relationship fell outside the boundaries of my youthful beliefs. I had the choice of either avoiding them or allowing the boundaries of my world to expand. Those are the exciting and frightening times when I painfully shed my religious exoskeleton to make way for a spiritual understanding that fit me better.

A crisis in faith may also be prompted by suffering: the death of a loved one, a life-threatening illness or injury, an assault, any event that falls far outside of what our belief system has prepared us for. When that happens, giving up our faith seems the only thing to do. Such experiences are like our spiritual exoskeleton getting ripped away. We are left raw and unprotected.

When a crisis of faith occurs, whether because of transition or tragedy, there are two important paths we can take. We can hold onto the faith of our childhood. This, however, means we must also hold onto our youthful view of the world, one that is simplistic and narrow. The other is to wait patiently and often painfully for a new understanding to develop, one that can provide meaning not only to the joy, but also to the complexity and suffering that inevitably come our way as we grow.

IN THE MEANTIME
November 12, 2008

In a recent conversation with a college senior, I listened as she lamented the bleak results of her job search. Her fear of not having a "real job" after graduation was building with each passing day. Then she continued with, "In the meantime," and went on to describe her plan to move from campus housing into an inexpensive apartment and to increase her part-time hours to make ends meet. This, she believed, would help her get through that undetermined stretch of time between graduation and a "real job." I admired her resourcefulness in the face of her fear and disappointment, and I told her so.

Her words, "In the meantime," got me thinking. Isn't that where much of life transpires? It's tempting to imagine that life will really begin once I get around the next corner. Once I get through with this project. Once I get that promotion, As soon as I get this debt paid off. Once my child graduates.

Yet, life continues to unfold while I am waiting, and what unfolds "in the meantime" is every bit as much of life as what I imagine I am waiting for. I have to remind myself that to wait "until" is to miss what's happening now, the only part of my life available to me. "In the meantime" continues to present us with all the challenge most of us need. We continue to face tragedies and causes for celebration, we experience gains and losses, we have tender and tense moments with loved ones during the days that pass "in the meantime."

This particular "meantime," nationally, internationally, financially, environmentally, and personally, seems to be characterized by crisis and conflict more than most times. The world around us seems to promote a crisis-oriented perspective. The media thrives on it, and the perspective becomes contagious. Before long, the crisis is all we can see. And experience teaches us that national and global crises intensify our personal dramas.

When we live with a crisis orientation, we are more often prompted by fear than by clear thinking. When that happens, our vision narrows and we lose sight of possibilities and resources. Living in the meantime does not mean being naively optimistic. Nor does it mean living in oblivion to what's going on. What we need is a full awareness of what's going on, which includes a bigger picture of not only the crisis but also the possibilities of how to live in the midst of crisis. Having a bigger picture allows us to acknowledge the fear but not be paralyzed by it.

We all live in the meantime. We have no choice. The task is to recognize it and make choices accordingly. Charlotte Joko Beck wrote, "We have sacrificed our life in this moment in order to think of things that are not present."

I frequently encountered a tangible example of this my psychology office at the university. Many college students sat in my office terrified that they were not going to do well on an important exam. They knew that their performance on the exam had implications for their overall grade, which in turn could potentially impact their degree and their future plans.

I always got the question, "How are you preparing for this exam?" Typically the students most terrified were the same ones who had not done the work during the semester and were not doing much to prepare for the exam. I stressed the principle: How you study for the exam tonight is a better predictor of your grade, and your future, than all the worry you can muster.

Are these global and personal crisis issues important? Absolutely. Do these issues deserve our best thoughts, efforts, and choices? Yes, indeed. Yet, how we live "in the meantime" is the best predictor of how we will deal with the crises as they unfold.

MEN AS MENTORS
February 8, 2009

Mark Twain observed that "at the age of twelve a boy starts imitating a man, and he just goes on doing that for the rest of his life." I suspect this is truer today than in Twain's day. There is no time or event or ritual that signifies a boy's entrance into manhood. Our culture provides no clear passage. Facial hair and pubic hair let a boy know he is developing physically and sexually. Becoming obstinate often signals an emotional pulling away from the family controls. But there are no clear road signs that declare when a boy has crossed the border into manhood. Of course, becoming a man is not an event. It is a process, and that process includes the modeling of manhood by other men.

Recently I had the honor of officiating at the home funeral and the graveside service of a man who was instrumental in that process for me. Ted was unlike the men I knew growing up, which made him all the more powerful. He was retired Air Force and physically imposing. He was generally quiet, but there was never a doubt he was in the room. His wisdom took up lots of space. We entered each other's lives more than 40 years ago. I was 26. He seemed ageless.

He was emotionally strong without being rigid. He was vulnerable, but it never came across as weakness. In fact, in his moments of vulnerability, his inner strength was on full display. He was open to all things, but careful and discerning in what he believed.

From my perspective, his life seemed full of adventure, travel, daring, and heavy responsibility. He learned lessons from his training and from war, and he shared those lessons in the form of stories. Yet his greatest service to me was to witness without judgment my struggles with growing into adulthood. The important words here are "witness without judgment." He listened to me with an open heart. He let me rant, whine, sulk, cry, and be utterly confused with my life. He provided no answers. What he provided was openness and support without any judgment. He knew the fear of being lost. He knew how easy it was to resort to anger or blaming when things didn't work out. He didn't let me get away with that. He knew I was tired of trying other people's ways of living. He'd been there before. He knew I had to find my own. He kept his hands symbolically, and sometimes literally, on my shoulders as I moved forward.

He also allowed me to witness his struggles. I saw his anger and frustration. I watched him cry and laugh. He let me in on his confusion about being a parent, a grandparent, a spouse, a son who had unfinished business with dead parents. In that way we moved together.

William Willimon expressed the grave concern, "It may be possible for a generation to move into adulthood with a minimum of adult interaction, but let the record show that we are the first culture to try it." He laments the fact that as a culture we provide few possibilities for personal, substantive interaction between boys and men; for boys "to look over the shoulders of adults and thereby get all the clues they can for adulthood." Without that we get grownup boys who spend their lives acting powerful while feeling powerless.

While fathers can provide crucial lessons for sons, the father-son relationship is often too convoluted for both to provide the clarity needed for mentoring into manhood. In fact, too often, the father is a grown boy still imitating a man. One of my deepest wishes is that somewhere, somehow, along the way my son finds someone like Ted to help him with the crucial tasks of becoming a man.

SEEING MOTHERS AS PEOPLE
May 9, 2011

It's Mother's Day.

In William Manchester's novel, **So Long, See You Tomorrow**, the main character makes the observation, "When my father was getting along in years, and the past began to figure more in his conversation, I asked him one day what my mother was like. I knew what she was like as my mother but I thought it was time somebody told me what she was like as a person."

It never occurred to me during my early years that my mother was a person, that she may have had a rich and interesting life before I was born, a childhood, teenage years, and a young adulthood before my brothers and I figured into the situation. She had an interesting life after we all left home as well, with friends and activities that had nothing to do with motherhood.

The middle part of her life was taken up with being a pastor's wife, something she had counted on, and being the mother of 5 boys, something she had not counted on. If she were alive today, she'd be 85 and very likely living an interesting life as a senior adult, the duties of motherhood in the distant past, but with countless stories of a motherhood she barely survived to fill her memory.

Mother's Day conjures up all kinds of memories and feelings. Of course, memories are never historically accurate. They are our own mixture of facts and interpretations. For most of us, memories of mother are tinted with bright colors and softened edges. But not for everyone. A friend of mine admitted some years ago that Mother's Day was not a good day for her. "My mother was mean. I have very few good memories." To her credit, my friend broke the cycle of meanness and became a good mother to her children.

I only saw my mother as competent, capable, and patient to a fault. It's hard for me to think of her as depressed, overwhelmed, sad, and lonely while she desperately tried to keep up with the constant onslaught of cooking, cleaning, laundry, and referee duties for the 5 of us, not to mention all of the public duties and social pressures as the pastor's wife. I know she experienced all those dark feelings. She didn't tell me, but I know.

I wonder if she ever found any consistent time to be alone, to be quiet, to look carefully at her life. I never asked her. I suspect she had some such moments shortly after the bunch of us dashed out the door to school and Dad headed off to the church office. I hope she pushed back the need to dive into her household duties long enough to have a cup of coffee and a quiet moment. But I don't know.

She was busy shaping my life and the lives of my brothers, quietly, subtly, maybe not even intentionally. She did it by making sure I had a breakfast in my stomach and a sack lunch in my hand before I left for school. I always had clean clothes, which I took for granted, and a hot dinner each evening, which I woofed down without much thought. She showed up for our little league games, which I doubt she wanted to do, and she was right there every evening making sure my homework was done and my teeth were brushed. Through those thankless tasks, and thousands more, she infused our home with a sense of emotional security.

The consistency with which she did these simple but difficult tasks was priceless. Consistency is far more important than flashy when it comes to rearing children.

For each of the past 7 years I have had the privilege of saying some things about my mother at a piano recital at Missouri Baptist University held in her memory. I get to tell the students and their parents some things about her as a mother and as a person. At the conclusion of the recital this year, one of the university administrators thanked me for my words. Without thinking I replied, "It's an honor. I get to say some things about her that I never got to say to her."

Happy Mother's Day, Mom.

FATHER AS A SPARRING PARTNER
July 3, 2011

I'm writing this on Father's Day. I just spent a week with my two young adult children, ages 29 and 22, who live in Illinois. I am now visiting my 85 year-old father on my return trip. I am experiencing multigenerational paternal whiplash.

I think my father was able to semi-retire from fatherhood within a few months of his last son leaving home for college. He's come out of retirement a few times as needed, but for many years he has been a father-emeritus, enjoying the benefits of his sons' successes without being pulled into our struggles.

I'm not yet there with my paternal duties. While I did not expect my job as a father to be done by now, I did not anticipate being called out of the bullpen quite as often and with so much riding on each pitch.

My daughter has just emerged from two years of total self-doubt. She borrowed a barrel of money to earn a master's degree that promised to pay off with a good job almost immediately. On approximately the same day she graduated, the economy collapsed.

Jobs in her field dried up. The promise was rescinded. There was weeping, wailing, and rending of vestments during those two years of marginal employment, resume revising, online searching, and fruitless interviewing.

My job during that time was that of emotional propper-upper. I did my best to remind her that patience and persistence were not just virtues but life skills, like treading water. I avoided statements about darkness and dawn. Clichés infuriate me when I'm feeling desperate. I reminded her that something would come, eventually. But when it's dark, it's hard to believe there is light anywhere.

Something did come. For the past four months, she almost giggles when she talks about her new job, even the steep learning curve, responsibilities, deadlines and long hours. All I do is nod, smile, and try not to burst.

My son has needed a different kind of propping up over the past couple of years. From my perspective, he's needed far more emotional support than he's been willing to receive and far less financial support than we've provided. Early in the visit this week I got a clearer picture of his living situation, his finances, and the way he spends his time and makes his decisions.

As people mature, they should become more effective at managing these basic aspects of life. While we can't control what life throws at us, we can learn to better manage those things that are within our control while life is busy throwing. He's been too willing to take easy paths in hopes of avoiding tough lessons. I was shoveling coal into a locomotive that was already out of control. I had to stop shoveling.

We had some tough talks. There was anger, tears (mine), lots of silence, and frequent acknowledgment of our deep affection for each other despite everything. My job was to be compassionate toward the 17 year-old that still lived inside him, and to be firm with the 22 year-old who was spiraling out of control. I felt mean when I got harsh with the scared and confused 17 year-old. I felt cowardly when I was soft on the insolent 22 year-old. As long as I kept those two separate in my mind and in the conversation, I was clear of my role.

Sometimes I think the role of the father is like the role of the sparring partner in boxing. A sparring partner is not the same as an opponent. The sparring partner is not there to defeat the other fighter but to match and challenge the skills of the other fighter. Hard blows are exchanged, but the purpose is not to knock out, injure, or demoralize.

The purpose is to make the aspiring boxer a better fighter. The sparring partner must know the fighter's strengths and weaknesses so they can focus on what needs work.

As a father, I have to be willing to stand toe to toe with my son, take his best punches, and not flinch. I also have to throw some punches, not to injure but to awaken. He's not yet as ready as he thinks he is for the fights ahead where punches are thrown to injure.

GOOD ENOUGH PARENTING
June 21, 2009

I'm writing this on Father's Day. My daughter, age 26, called me from the east coast where she is engaged in a graduate program summer internship. My 19 year-old son called on a borrowed cell phone because he hasn't paid his phone bill for the past 3 months. It would be easy to look at the obvious and decide to be proud of one and disappointed with the other. But as parents, we know there's more to it than that.

They are different kids, different ages, and they bring such different things to the table. Given the circumstances that go way beyond the obvious, I can't imagine being more proud of each one. With each of my kids I have had moments of feeling like a total failure as a parent. Fortunately, I've had far more moments of speechless gratitude and breath-taking respect for each of them.

"Bring up a child in the way he should go," is still an important proverb, but the conclusion, "and when he is old he will not depart from it" is no longer a given. When this was written, communities were more religiously and culturally homogeneous. Intergenerational families lived in the same town or even in the same house, and friends lived as neighbors through their whole life. Religion, education, and family history were intertwined in the normal course of life, and kids could rarely escape the eyes and ears of all those corrective influences.

Such is not the case today. Our society is mobile and diverse, and children are influenced daily in ways unimaginable just a generation ago. More and more of their lives beyond the age of 12 are lived outside the awareness of parents. The internet and smart phones, which were not realities when I was growing up, allow children and teens to access information and engage in relationships and activities that are completely independent of their family, school, and church life.

This and many other influences make parenting a more important and a more difficult job than ever before. We are bombarded with advice from parenting experts through books, newspaper articles, and television shows, but there are few clear guidelines for how to prepare our kids for experiences that will undoubtedly be far beyond their maturity level. And, of course, children always think their maturity level is far beyond our assessment.

In the face of all this, there are no perfect parents. All we can strive for as parents are the patience, persistence, daring, and good humor to be a "good-enough" parent.

We know we're making it up as we go, bluffing much of the time. All we have to go on is what we experienced from our parents, who were far from perfect, and from watching other parents, also flawed. Yet, we live and work in a culture that promotes the idea that we should know what we're doing, we should be certain and confident, and we should be capable of rising to any demand.

As parents we've lived long enough to know that's not true or possible, but how are we as parents supposed to admit that to our children? How do we admit we don't know, we're not sure, we make mistakes, we get scared?

I have to start by reminding myself that there are no perfect fathers or mothers, that being a "good enough" parent is often the best I can do. To me, that means two things: being clear with myself about my intentions, what do I want for my kids? Then, making sure those intentions are communicated in my words and visible in my actions.

What I hope for my children is that they possess an inquisitive mind, a tender heart, a strong moral intuition, a sense of personal responsibility, and the capacity to endure disappointment. If that's what I want for them, if those are my intentions, I need to make sure they see those qualities in me, consistently, daily, over the course of years through all the normal, routine activities of family living and growing up.

Most of the time, "good enough" is enough.

THE DINER
July 25, 2014

I visited an old friend a couple of weeks ago. I've known her since 1984. We visited together at least once each week until she moved away from Urbana, Illinois in 2002. She moved to a small town near Schenectady, New York and changed her name. I knew her as the Elite Diner. Now she's the Chuck Wagon.

I traveled about 1800 miles to see her. According to the map, she was just a few miles off the road on my trip to Maine, so it seemed a good detour. Turns out it was a great detour. She was just as I'd remembered her. Silver with red trim, the rounded corners, windows across the front. The Elite. A 50's diner beautifully refurbished.

For the 18 years I had known her, she and her tiny parking lot had lived on a cramped corner in downtown Urbana. She looks bigger now that she lives in a larger space. She had not changed much on the inside, either. Same green and pink tiles on the floor with the same cracks in the tiles. The same silver, pink, and green on walls and ceiling, same booths, though reupholstered.

I sat on the same stool at the counter I had occupied hundreds of times. Sometimes I sat by myself, sometimes one of my children was on a stool next to me. The same green Formica counter, the seam in the Formica rubbed smooth from thousands of plates of food and mugs of coffee sliding over it.

I had spent hundreds of hours of writing, thinking, planning, or just gathering my early-morning thoughts. I'd had meetings with colleagues and bosses there. I'd commiserated with Bob the welder who also had an infant son at the time. We'd compared hours of sleep or lack thereof from the night before.

But mostly, this became the place I shared with my kids. This was where we connected over coffee and hot chocolate, sometimes a sweet roll, sometimes a Number 9 (an unhealthy but totally satisfying plate of biscuits covered with hash browns and sausage gravy). My children, now 32 and 25, never hesitated if I woke them before dawn, two hours before their school started, as long as my question was, "Want to go to the Diner?"

Once at the counter, sometimes we talked, sometimes we just sat. We listened to the music overhead and I talked about (or made up stuff about) the oldies playing and what was going on with me when the song was new. We watched and evaluated the cook as he did his magic with the eggs, pancakes, bacon, or whatever was on the griddle directly in front of us. "Don't pat the pancakes after you turn them," I admonished them. That's one of my cardinal rules of breakfast cooking. It's also a pretty good metaphor for lots of things in life. We watched and frowned at each other if the cook did it.

I was sitting on this very stool the morning my daughter and I had a falling out that ended our trips to the Diner for a few years. It was a sad but necessary morning for each of us. One of parenting's tough tasks is to set limits and to teach them to deal with disappointment. That was one of those morning we each learned lessons we didn't want, but needed.

Each stool and booth had soaked up thousands of moments that were so common, so mundane, that, at the time, it was easy to miss how immensely important and formative they were. But as I sat there this past week, enjoying my coffee and breakfast, the naugahyde and aluminum gave back some of those memories.

As I left, I paused and patted the first stool at the counter. Twenty-five years earlier I sat my son's car seat on that stool while I paid my bill. He was in it. I don't know if he moved or if I bumped it, but he and the car seat crashed to the hard tile floor. He was startled, but fine. Everyone else was rattled. He became the focus of attention the next few times I brought him in. By the time he was old enough to order for himself, the staff knew him by name.

As I passed through her front door to leave, I patted her door frame, told her good-bye, that I'd probably never see her again, that I was glad I'd made this trip and was glad she was holding up so well.

A few days later, over Father's Day dinner with my children, I realized it was in that place I learned a great deal about being a father. I got to practice there over coffee and a Number 9. And as is true in much of life, there is no difference between practice and living.

LEAVING, LEARNING, GRIEVING
August 25, 2014

Several years ago I was leading a panel discussion for parents of incoming college freshmen. The topic of the moment was "Move-in day." One of the parents on the panel had just told a detailed, emotionally wrenching story of leaving her daughter at the college dorm and crying all the way back home. Many in the audience of 400 dabbed their eyes with Kleenex as she finished.

I knew this would not be the experience for most, so after a long silence, I broke in with the question, "How many of you are like me. You had a daughter who was a dream for the first 15 years, and then spent her high school years making it real easy for me to say 'Good-bye' to her when I took her to college?" Relieved chuckles rippled through the crowd, a majority of hands went up, heads nodded, and one man near the front gave an audible, "Oh God, yes!"

Those big moments of change never come with just one emotion. It's always a mixed bag of sadness, elation, relief, fear, and a host of other thoughts and feelings. Many parents here and throughout the nation have recently left their son or daughter at college. For many students it's their first time to truly leave home for an extended time. For many parents it's the biggest "letting go" so far. Now what?

One of the useful ways of thinking about these changes is by thinking about loss and the grief that follows. We often think of grief only in relation to the bereavement following a death, but in fact, life is a series of grief experiences. Each movement forward in life carries with it the loss of something familiar. Even those turning points we usually characterize as happy events have mixed within them elements of grief. Whether it's leaving home for the very first day of Kindergarten or leaving home years later to go to college, the excitement of what's ahead is always mingled with the feelings that go with loss.

Each student and each parent will respond to these transitions differently, because each person's experience is their own unique constellation of thoughts and feelings. For many of your students, their experiences at the university will contain a workable balance of challenges and supports, and the net result is a good-enough social, emotional, and academic adjustment to the university. The same can be said of your adjustment to life without your child at home.

For other students, however, the challenges will outweigh the supports. When this happens, the students can feel overwhelmed, lonely, or lost for a while. This is the time when you as a parent may get a tearful, desperate phone call. "I hate this place! I can't get along with my roommate! My classes are awful! I don't belong here!" One of my former colleagues confessed that she got that call from her son exactly 35 minutes after she let him off at the dorm.

If that happens, **don't panic.** It may take some time, some listening and talking to determine if the situation is truly desperate or if those are the normal reactions to the loss of the familiar and the anxiety of the not-yet-familiar.

Remember that your young child-adult is learning a lot these first weeks, and only a small part of that learning is happening in the classroom. In fact, only a small part of it is happening in their awareness.

They are learning about the extent and the limits of their abilities, about managing new responsibilities for all kinds of things in their lives, about community living, values, decision-making, and all the other things that go with new independence.

These are daunting tasks that only get resolved with time, patience, support, and trial and error. In some situations, they'll need help from residence advisors, instructors, academic advisors, or counselors. Parents, make sure they know about these resources, and encourage them to use them.

Every transition, particularly the painful ones, provides an opportunity to learn some valuable lessons and develop some important life skills, for them and for you. Helping your daughter or son navigate their own way through the tough times, rather than quickly bailing them out, allows you to be a part of their lessons.

What do parents need? Patience, a willingness to listen, to hold your tongue, to encourage them to take the actions they need to take on their own behalf, and to point them to the appropriate resources.

They are busy learning lots of new things. As a parent, so are you.

GRIEF AT AN EARLY AGE
August 15, 2010

As I stood silently, my candle in hand, I looked around at the faces of about a hundred twenty-somethings at the candlelight vigil. The evening air was heavy with sadness as they gathered to commemorate the life and death of their friend. Her death was tragic. She was pulled from a house fire too late. She survived for a few weeks, but her burns were too severe. Now, two weeks after her death, many at the vigil still looked stunned. You could almost see their thoughts at work, trying to make some kind of sense of it all.

The death of a teenager or young adult is always a tragedy. There is no way to spin it that makes it anything less. No matter the circumstances, a young life coming to an end makes no sense. No explanation softens the reality; no rhyme or reason can make it OK. Whether by illness, accident, or suicide, death at an early age is tragic and always leaves young survivors reeling.

For many of those standing there, I suspect this was their first experience of the death of someone so close to them, so close to their own age. This will be a turning point for them. They will mark their lifelines as "Before her death" and "After her death." For others, it is yet another significant loss. For my son, standing in their midst, it is his third loss in as many years.

Most of the experts on grief say that the first steps in healing are to acknowledge the loss and to experience the pain. I doubt anyone in the group had been instructed on the process of grief. Yet here they were, intuitively or out of sheer need, their candles burning, acknowledging their loss and feeling their intense pain and confusion in the presence of each other.

Most were dressed in their characteristic black, they were tattooed and pierced and spiked. They live on the fringes of the world I inhabit and they seem clueless about so many things that are essential to my middle-aged, middle class professional world. Yet, they were engaged in a group wisdom. Somehow they knew that grief is more bearable and more healing when shared with those who are also grieving. Many at the vigil had been together daily since their friend's death. A few in attendance had been rescued from the fire that took her life, and now they were standing in the front yard of that house, looking at each other and up at her second-story window, charred and boarded up.

This young woman's life, like many of those standing in the yard, had a trajectory that was clearly forward and upward. She was working to support her siblings while also saving for college. She was building friendships that were going to last forever. She was living her life with all the gusto, drama, joy, and pain that any young adult experiences. Her death throws all sorts of existential confusion at the survivors. It calls into question the purpose and meaning of life itself at a time when life should hold so much promise and possibility. It calls into question their own mortality at a time when they feel physically invulnerable.

I learned long ago from my own grief and from helping others with their grief, that you can't take away the pain of grief. It's a given. You can, however, by being together, by talking and laughing and crying together, even by standing in silence together, take away some of the fear and the loneliness that comes with the pain.

They have figured out on their own that isolation inhibits healing. There are no answers to be found, but togetherness helps. Huddling together is often the best way to hold on until we regain our footing and can take our next step.

As I stood there with my candle, dusk settled and the sky gradually darkened. Those of us who happened to look up at the right moment saw a shooting star. It was bright and fast, and then it was gone.

THE DEATH OF A BROTHER
December 4, 2012

As I sat in the memorial service for my friend, Hal, my attention kept drifting to Hal's only brother, Dale. He was sitting a few rows in front of me, on the aisle of the second row, the section reserved for the family. He was in his late 70's, had thinning hair, and had been reduced in size by illness over the past few years.

There was no mention of him in the service. I doubt it was intentional. It's just that in a memorial service, the spouse, the children, the grandchildren, and close friends get most of the mention. Somehow the surviving members of the family of origin frequently go unnoticed. Having brothers myself, I was aware of the omission and imagined the emptiness he was feeling.

Following the service, as everyone milled about snacking on punch and cookies, I spotted Dale. He knew lots of the people there and had been moving from one group to another talking to friends and family. But now he was standing alone, looking a little lost. I approached him and though I had met him before, I introduced myself.

There is no right thing to say, so I started with what I had been thinking. "I can't imagine many things any harder than losing a brother."

His eyes rimmed with tears and he replied, "Yeah, it's pretty hard."

I told him how sorry I was for his loss, and then added, "You have known Hal longer than anyone in this building." I could as easily have said, "than anyone in the world," for he was the last of his family of origin.

"Yes I did. Thank you."

I wanted to unburden my heart, to talk about how hard it must be to lose a person you had played with and fought with since you were young boys, but that would have been for my benefit, not his. So we exchanged a few more words, I don't remember what they were, and I excused myself. I was humbled by his loss, unique from anyone else's in the room.

I grew up assuming that our affection for our siblings just somehow gets channeled into affection for our spouse and children. That seemed to be the model I observed in my parents. Neither of them spoke of their brothers and sisters as if they were current relationships that continued to grow and evolve. Maybe they did, but I didn't see it or hear about it. I grew up with the impression that my aunts and uncles were people who were part of my parents' past and people we visited on vacations.

Longitudinal sociological and psychological studies have repeatedly shown that sibling relationships are among the most important in our lives, even if they don't stay in touch later in life. Sibling relationships are important because they are so formative in making us the adults we are today. Our siblings are our first peer relationships. With them we learn to play, fight, negotiate, share possessions, share secrets. We learn much about who we are based on our interactions with those who live under the same roof and often in the same room.

Fortunately, my brothers and I decided many years ago that our relationships were worth nurturing and building on. We knew how to be kids together, but it took us some years to learn how to be adults together. My brothers are among my most rewarding, challenging, and evolving relationships. The way I see the world and the way I see myself would be greatly diminished had we settled years ago for just being boys together. My adult relationships with my brothers have been life-changing.

A couple of years ago I was talking with another friend prior to the funeral of his brother. My friend had been a minister and teacher his whole career. He had conducted hundreds of funerals, many for his own relatives. He told me, "I performed the services for my mom and my dad. But I couldn't do my brother's service."

"Of course you couldn't," was my only reply. Some things are just too sacred and tender and deep.

INCLUSION/DIVERSITY

When Barack Obama was elected president in 2008, many proclaimed that our country had entered the post-racism era. To the contrary, the racism that had been neatly tucked beneath the surface of our national psyche came out. Hate crimes increased in frequency and intensity. As legislation expanded rights to women, people of color, and LGBT groups, overt expressions of hatred and violence toward these groups increased. The grip of white privilege was loosening, but not without a fight.

The grip of white privilege has tightened once again in the past few years. History slowly moves toward greater inclusion. Diversity in its many forms adds to the collective wisdom of our culture and our world, but this inclusion will continue to face opposition from those diminishing numbers who fear losing their institutional privilege and their illusion of supremacy.

TAKING WHICH COUNTRY BACK?
February 28, 2016

"We're going to take our country back!" That has been a rallying cry for Republicans for the past several years. It underlies the Presidential race and was a prevalent theme of the Taylor County Republican forum a few weeks ago as candidates for county, state, and national offices introduced themselves to the eager crowd.

At the forum there was plenty of talk of what each would do if elected, lots of praise for current Republicans in office, most notably Governor Abbot, and plenty of bashing Democrats for what has been done or not done. It was energetic, uplifting, and congenial for all the like-minded people there.

While "taking our country back" certainly gets the juices going for many, what does it mean? Back from whom? Some of the answers to that question are clear, some are more illusive.

Taking our country back from a Supreme Court that gave to gays and lesbians the same civil rights enjoyed by married heterosexuals was one clear theme. Also, it's crucial that we take it back from non-Christians who have made it illegal for Christians to put the Ten

Commandments and Nativity scenes wherever we choose. That pesky First Amendment.

We have to take it back from invaders who are seeking refuge from life-threatening situations, not unlike what many of our great-grandparents did. We're taking it back from a President who some still believe is a Muslim who hates this country. Yes, amazingly, some people still believe he's Muslim. One of our state candidates actually said, with a straight face, that the president is intentionally trying to ruin this country. Many applauded. The list of groups we can blame for highjacking our country is long.

And back to what? Back to when? If we take back what has transpired over the past few years or the past few decades, whose civil rights should we revoke? Women? People of color? Gays and lesbians, some of whom are our family members, friends, and colleagues? Muslim citizens? The disabled? Those who cannot afford health care? To whom will we say, "You can no longer enjoy the civil liberties you have fought so hard for. Sorry, but we want it back the way it was before we had to take you seriously."

And who is "we?" It's people like me. White, heterosexual, male, Christian, able-bodied, born-in-America Americans. People who have the privileges that come with being born into those kinds of families. People who, compared to other kinds of families, had fewer hurdles to jump over to go to college or get a job. We who are still in charge but don't feel like it as much.

The truth is, the country we want back is a country known only to a small portion of us. Many others living within the same borders of this great land have known little or nothing of the country we want back.

However, the country we think we want back is not likely to return, and it's not the fault of those we'd like to blame. The world has moved forward, and we are experiencing the inevitable pains of that growth and change.

For example, our country has always been multicultural and multiracial, but we just started taking that seriously the past few decades. Women have always deserved the same rights, privileges, and choices as men, but we're still having trouble with that one. The world's countries are more interconnected and interdependent than ever before. While we can still boast the best military and strongest economy, we can no longer stand alone militarily or economically. The rules have changed.

We say we want to restore Christian values, but we have simplistically redefined Christian values as alignment with particular political issues. These have little resemblance to Christ-like values such as humility, compassion, forgiveness, peace-making, and being of service to the least of these.

Are we on a slippery slope? Some use that analogy to describe what has happened in terms of our values, policies, and laws. I have to remember that what seems like a slippery slope to me may in fact be a movement toward equality for others.

We in the majority have some privileges that put us above the fray. Any movement toward equality with those who have not shared our privileges may feel like we're the one being oppressed.

What seems like a slippery slope may in fact simply be sliding from my position of privilege onto a level playing field with other citizens of this great country, a movement toward "justice for all."

WHITE PRIVILEGE
October 4, 2009

When Jimmy Carter made the assertion that the intense animosity shown lately toward President Obama is based on racism, he stirred some people up. Some dismissed him, others sat up and took notice. Here's a past president making a bold statement. Whatever the reaction, Carter has once again raised the issue of race as an underlying, yet powerful force at work in our nation.

Many of us have difficulty identifying with the charge of "racism." We think of racism as the blatant, close-minded, hate-filled type we see and hear in white supremacists. We're not like that. We're more informed, open-minded, and civil than those people.

However, my racism and the racism I observe around me are just as damaging, if not more so. Subtle and insidious, my brand of racism rarely invites honest exchange, introspection, or action. It can pass as condescending tolerance at its most benign, or as fearful hostility in its more destructive expressions.

What are we to make of the faces and the voices of otherwise mild-mannered, middle-class, middle-aged folks screaming at town hall meetings, tea parties, and talk radio? What can we make of the movements and messages aimed against the president? The birther movement, efforts to paint Obama as a Muslim, a socialist, a Communist, a Nazi, as someone who will euthanize old people and brainwash our kids through his education speech. All of these portray him as "not one of us."

The cries to "take back our country", by force if necessary, is not just protesting Obama's policies and plans. The cry is promoting the idea that we are losing our country to someone who is not one of us. The "us" is code for "those whom we have always known to be in power."

The noise and hostility, at least in part, appears to be those of us who have always been in charge now fearing that we are losing or have already lost the privileges that come with being in charge. You know, us white guys.

Multicultural literature speaks of those who are "targets" and those who are "privileged." The targets are those in the minority, whatever that minority might be. They live without many of the societal, cultural, formal or informal power that the privileged enjoy. The privileged often don't even recognize their privilege, because it just comes with the territory. It's in the air we breathe from birth.

Being a White, heterosexual male, for example, I never have to worry if my skin color is going to get me unwelcomed attention when I enter a store, stroll through a public building, or walk in a white neighborhood. I can go into my bank dressed in my grubbiest working clothes and never be asked to produce more than the basic identification for any transaction. If I speak up in a group, I don't worry that if I say something stupid, it will be attributed to my race, or if I say something notable, I will be considered a credit to my race. Yet, these are common experiences my African-American students and friends have talked about.

We in the white majority rarely think about the degree to which our history, our news, our laws, and every part of our lives are a reflection of the majority culture. Those who are the target groups rarely forget it.

Justice Sotomayor's confirmation highlighted this reality. Many in the Senate and around the nation accused her of racism when she stated that no one could fully separate their culture from their perspective and decision-making, even in matters of the law. We were astonished. How can the law be a matter of cultural perspective? Yet, because the Supreme Court has always been overwhelmingly Caucasian and male, those of us who are Caucasian and have grown up in a male-dominated society had no reason to think about the law being interpreted through culture. Ours was always well represented.

Differences of opinion about political issues are not new. But the level of hostility being expressed indicates there's more going on, and I suspect it's coming from those in the majority who fear losing their foothold of power.

CHANGING HEARTS AND MINDS
October 15, 2011

Written during the 2012 presidential campaign.
Mitt Romney was challenging Barack Obama.

"Poisonous language doesn't soften anybody's heart, it doesn't change anybody's mind." This was Mitt Romney's response to the verbal attack on his faith. So what does soften someone's heart or change someone's mind?

I was one of four people being interviewed on a radio program a few years ago. The topic was homosexuality and the church. It was not a debate, but rather an exploration of why churches had such difficulty being accepting of homosexuality.

We each talked about difficulties of our own denominations in making policy and doctrinal decisions about homosexuality. I talked about the deep rift in my denomination, Presbyterian.

We also talked about personal histories related to the topic. I grew up Southern Baptist in East Texas at a time when homosexuality was rarely talked about. If it was mentioned at all it was in pitying terms. In high school and college, being called a "queer" was the consummate insult. We never considered that anyone among us was actually gay, so making jokes about it was easy and impersonal.

The radio host then asked me, "What makes this personal for you?" What did make this personal for me? I was momentarily stumped. My views had changed considerably over the years. How had that change come about? I took a few seconds to formulate a careful rationale, but then I realized there was nothing particularly rational about the changes. They were more emotional and personal than rational.

"I got to know someone. I grew to respect her as a professional and grew to love her as a person. She is lesbian, and being lesbian is a big part of what makes her the person I love and respect."

There it was. My change of mind and heart was the result of a relationship. Of course, this realization was many years in the making. One of my closest friends in college was gay, though I did not know it at the time. He talked of his struggles and personal anguish years later.

Some of the people I worked with in therapy had come out as gay or lesbian during our work together, and I admired their courage and wisdom in moving from scared and closeted to out, open, and at peace. They struggled with the same life issues I struggled with, such as money, life direction, family, intimacy, but they often had to do it in secret, without the support of friends, family, or their church.

Every one of us knows and respects someone who is gay or lesbian. If you have more than a handful of acquaintances, coworkers, or extended family, you know someone who is gay or lesbian. If you think you don't know anyone who identifies as homosexual, that's because those friends, coworkers, and family members haven't felt safe enough to tell you.

But this principle of relational change is not confined to sexual orientation. This is a universal principle. The turning point in so many issues today has to be relational. As long as we can put someone in a category, identify them by a single issue, or lump them into a group, we can then judge them by whatever stereotypes we wish, and then dismiss them.

"Oh, he's a Mormon, she's a Republican, he's gay, she's Pro-Choice, he's an illegal..." Labeling allows me to see someone as less than a full person. It narrows my perspective and reduces my capacity to think, understand, and grow. It makes my world smaller.

We will not become "a more prefect union" through debates, research, rational arguments, or yelling. Our political intolerance and gridlock as well as our cultural, racial, and religious conflicts will continue until we make it relational. This does not mean we have to agree with those who hold opposing views, but it does mean we must see "the other" as a person who has a great deal to teach us simply by being who they are. A friend of mine on occasions calls people who have written letters to the editor that he profoundly disagrees with. He invites them for coffee just to talk and try to understand their point of view.

When I asked why he did that, he simply replied, "It's just so interesting. I always learn something." Now that's a relational approach.

CRUEL CONCLUSIONS
November 30, 2014

When I was first learning to write, I obediently positioned my paper on my desk according to the teacher's instructions. But when I wrote, unlike my classmates, I crooked my hand around so that I was essentially writing upside down. The teacher was teaching us as if we were all right-handers. I'm left-handed.

Not many years ago it was common for parents and teachers to try to 'break' small children of using their left hand, to convert them to be right-handers, thinking it would be better for them in the long run. In some classrooms left-handed children were punished by having their left hand tied behind their chair or by having their left hand smacked with a ruler or yardstick. My teachers did not try to break me. They simply ignored my struggle.

Children were treated as if they willfully chose to be left-handed and simply needed to be converted to right-handedness.

The decision to use one hand instead of the other for most tasks is automatic, not conscious. We pick up a pen to write. We grip a golf club. It's not taught. It's not a willful act. It's not a statement. It is innate. We know this now and accept this without questioning, but it has not always been so.

Throughout history faulty assumptions about left-handedness were imbedded in the culture. Left-handedness was historically seen as a sign of evil, pathology, or perversion in many cultures. Even the Bible portrayed the righteous being on the right, the evil on the left. They adopted prejudice that existed in other cultures at that time.

None of this was based on any real scientific knowledge, but solely on the fact that a minority group exhibited a behavior that seemed abnormal to the right-handed majority. Therefore, the legal, scientific, and religious experts of the day attributed malicious intent to the behavior they did not understand.

It was not until Paul Broca's discoveries about the lateralization of the brain in the late 19th century that scientific interest in handedness began. Serious scientific study of brain lateralization and handedness did not begin to flourish until the 1970s.

With experience and accurate information, our culture and institutions now see left-handedness not as willful behavior, but as a normal way of being for approximately 10% of the population.

Yet, even today in some places in the world, people are discouraged, even forbidden from and punished for using their left hand. You can't forbid someone from being left-handed. You can stifle the use of their left hand, but they are still left-handed by nature.

Cruel conclusions are always drawn when people confuse innate behavior and willed behavior.

Our culture is finally coming to the same understanding of being gay or lesbian. We now know that homosexuality is not a chosen "lifestyle." A person doesn't will himself or herself to be homosexual any more than most of us will ourselves to be attracted to the opposite sex.

Sexual orientation is an innate part of who we are as humans. It is a part of our biology. Non-heterosexuals make up about 10% of the population. They have always been part of our mainstream culture. They've always been our friends and in our families. But now they are more visible and vocal.

And yet in our culture, many forms of discrimination are still common and in some cases condoned, including firings, bullying, beatings, disinheriting, even killings by strangers, acquaintances, even families.

Programs exist that are aimed at converting homosexuals to something that is natural to most of us, but unnatural to them. Conversion therapy, one such program outlawed in many states, seeks to change a homosexual into a heterosexual, usually using punitive Christian principles. Such programs can, in some cases, suppress their natural inclinations and their behavior. However, with the right kind of punishment, fear, and brainwashing, you could do the same with heterosexuals, but it always comes at a steep emotional cost.

Each of us has close friends or family members who are gay, lesbian, or bisexual. They may have chosen not to be open about it, but if you have any kind of extended family or circle of friends, you care deeply about someone who is homosexual. As a community that values freedom of expression and individual liberties, it's time we make this a safer place for them to be who they are.

"ARE YOU A RACIST?"
April 30, 2014?

In April 2014, Donald Sterling, owner of NBA's Los Angeles Clippers, was banned from the NBA following the release of private recordings between Sterling and his mistress that contained racist comments. Locally, a group of college students were arrested for racist graffiti on campus. Once again, racism was headline news.

"Are you a racist?" That was a question shouted by a reporter to Donald Sterling as the L.A. Clipper's owner headed for his car. It's a provocative question, but it's the wrong question for Sterling, and it's the wrong question for each of us. Except in cases where a person is hateful enough or ignorant enough to want to be identified as a racist, the question does not lend itself to a "Yes/No" answer. Racism is not an all-or-nothing situation. It's not a switch you turn off once you are no longer a racist.

The better questions for each of us might be, "How do your racial biases affect the way you think about others?" "In what ways do your racial biases show themselves in your actions?" "When do you recognize and knowingly condone institutional racism?" Those kinds of questions suddenly bring us all in on the conversation.

It takes the arrogance of a Donald Sterling, the ignorance of a Cliven Bundy, or the immaturity of a recent group of local college students to bring race back to the headlines, but it never goes away from our daily lives.

Malcolm Gladwell, in his book, **Blink,** describes the Implicit Association Test, developed by three Harvard psychologists. The test measures our conscious attitudes on a number of dimensions, including race. Conscious attitudes are those things we choose to believe. These are the attitudes and beliefs we can articulate, and they typically guide our deliberate behaviors.

Beyond that, however, the test does a frighteningly effective job of measuring our unconscious attitudes, those immediate, automatic associations that pop into our heads or tumble out of our mouths before we've had time to think. We don't deliberately choose these attitudes and may not be aware that they are even there. According to Gladwell, "The disturbing thing about the test is that it shows that our unconscious attitudes may be utterly incompatible with our stated conscious values."

If you grew up in this country and are old enough to read this article, regardless of your race or ethnicity, you have absorbed racist beliefs and stereotypes, and they have shaped your life and outlook. It's part of the air we breathe, and it is endemic in every institution in our society. The question is not, "Are you a racist?" The question is, "How much do you recognize your racial biases? How complicit are you in the many forms of institutional racism?"

Those are not judgmental questions, because they address aspects of ourselves that are as much who we are as our bones and noses. The object is to become aware of those parts.

In the midst of a recent casual conversation, a local businessman uttered a despicable slur regarding our President. I was stunned. I had been lulled into believing that intelligent, respectable people don't say such things about any other human being, no matter how much they may disagree with them. With the bar lowered to that level, it would be easy to excuse myself with the assurance of, "At least I'm not like that guy." But we each have to deal with our own conscious and unconscious racism. We all participate overtly or in silence.

And it isn't just about Blacks and Whites. The recent shooting in Kansas by the White supremacist reminds us of the mean, cruel, and sometimes deadly nature of intolerance toward any group.

Using the word such as "racist" or "homophobe" makes the issue too simple. Such words dichotomize things and people, and once divided into categories, we can say, "I'm not one of those." But it's not that simple. Intolerance is rooted in ignorance, produces fear, and is often acted out in hateful words and actions. We all participate, and we all suffer. Intolerance sometimes kills the body, but it always damages the spirit, first and foremost of the person who is afraid and acting out of that fear. And that includes each of us.

INSTITUTIONAL RACISM
IN THE CURRICULUM
March 10, 2010

Like most people, I went through school thinking that history was history was history. Events happened on specific dates, certain people were involved, and that was that. I was primarily concerned about learning the facts that would give me a passing grade. I thought little about the social and political context or consequences of those historical events.

I did not realize that history was not just about facts. It is also about perspective. The telling of history is a personal and political activity, because history is always told through the experience and perspective of the teller. What I learned about world history, American history, and Texas history was as much an interpretation as it was a description, whether the interpretation came from a book or from a story told on the front porch.

The recent standards adopted by the Texas state board of education for the teaching of history, economics, and social studies is a clear example of how perspective shapes facts. According to a variety of news sources, the final standards that have been adopted represent the views and values of one faction, conservatives. They were chosen over the views and values of another faction, mostly moderates, including racial minorities. To no one's surprise, those factions tended to divide down political lines of Republican and Democrat.

What that means is that our students will be learning a history that, according to board member, Mary Helen Berlanga, has been "whitewashed." It's also been Christianized and de-liberalized. For example, students will learn more about the Christian influences in our nation's history and less about the founding principle of religion freedom. Joe McCarthy will be made more credible. The Moral Majority and the conservative resurgence in the 1980s and 90s will be treated as important historical phenomena. Phyllis Schlafly's influence in that resurgence will be included, but the influence of Thomas Jefferson's writings during the American Revolution will not.

When you have a group advocating one narrow perspective on history, a lot of influential people and a lot of important views get downplayed or eliminated, and a lot of important history that has shaped our state and nation gets ignored.

This is not a new battle. Noted American historian, John Hope Franklin, in his autobiography, "Mirror to America," described a similar situation in 1966 when he and some colleagues were invited to write a history text for consideration by the California board of education. Their text included information about how slavery, a 400-year period in our history, had shaped our national story. The book also described the civil rights movement, still in its early stages, as an important extension of that long, painful history.

The response was dramatic. "In some communities," he wrote, "a veritable tug-of-war broke out between groups that advocated a more celebratory, which to them meant patriotic, past, and those that sought a more critical approach, encouraging a diversity of opinion and value in the belief that this would teach tolerance." A publicity campaign was waged against Franklin accusing him of being un-American, and his textbook was ultimately rejected.

It appears we haven't come very far in Texas in the intervening 44 years. The new standards appear to be a celebration of the conservative White Christian perspective of our country.

In an act of tragic irony, the board deleted a sociology requirement that high school students "explain how institutional racism is evident in American society." Institutional racism is the network of institutional and societal structures, policies, practices and behaviors (in this case public education) that intentionally or unintentionally create advantages and benefits for one group of people (in this case white Christians) and disadvantages and hindrances for other groups. Such racism is rarely seen and therefore easily dismissed by those whose position is advantaged. Those who are disadvantaged, misrepresented, or even omitted see it clearly and routinely.

By eliminating from the curriculum an exploration of "institutional racism", the school board has presented us all with a crystal clear example of it.

MEN, LET'S ERR ON
THE SIDE OF IGNORANCE
November 11, 2017

The "#Me too" movement has been sobering for me to watch. A number of my female friends, former colleagues, and family members have used social media to speak out about their own experiences of sexual harassment, assault, or rape. Those two simple words, "Me too," have revealed how pervasive the problem is in every institution and in every corner of our society. The problem has been there all along, but we have generally ignored it. By "we" I mean men like me.

We have been willing to turn our heads when sexual harassment or assault made headlines. We shook our heads in sad disbelief as Bill Cosby denied charges brought by more than a dozen women. Then, when it was no longer front-page news, we stopped thinking about it. We chuckled when our soon-to-be president bragged in disgusting detail about his own inappropriate sexual behavior. Many glibly chalked it up to locker room talk and voted for him anyway.

It took a Harvey Weinstein to finally create momentum as more than two dozen women, many of whom we have admired in their movie roles, spoke up about his predatory sexual behavior over the past 20 years. Once the women Weinstein had targeted started coming forward, others did the same. The "Me too" campaign took flight and allegations and reports came from every direction; against bosses, co-workers, CEOs, neighbors, everywhere.

Now we as a culture, and particularly we as men, have an important decision. We can take this seriously or we can forget about it as soon as it's no longer on the evening news. Weinstein is an easy target for our outrage. He is from Hollywood. Those who want to dismiss the issue can say, "Well, it's Hollywood. What do you expect?" Those who want to use it for political or religious ammunition can say, "That's the Hollywood elite. We're not like that." We can all find some way to dismiss this social epidemic.

The hard part will be to continue to recognize it, stand up to it, call it what it is, or simply stop doing it. The temptation will be to dismiss the reality that sexual harassment and assault take place in every institution in our country. It happens in businesses large and small, local and global; in churches large and small; in the halls of local, state, and national government; in civic groups, in families.

Sexual harassment happens in the workplace, but it also happens in the grocery store, in the hallways at school, during staff meetings, while having coffee with friends. Anywhere and anytime an unwelcomed behavior, statement, or gesture of a sexual nature is made, it has happened again. Someone has been demeaned because of her gender and we have all been diminished because it still plays such a prominent role in our culture.

The simplest way to dismiss this reality is by assuming that every woman who has ever felt slighted is now claiming sexual harassment. We roll our eyes and rationalize that this is the latest form of whining, blaming, and jumping on the bandwagon. I have already heard that argument in recent conversations. This heaps insult on top of tragedy.

If we (men) are going to err, let's err on the side of believing women. Let's err on the side of assuming we don't understand and we need to learn some things. Let's err on the side of assuming it happens all around us, even to the women we love and respect, and we don't see it. Let's err on the side of taking responsibility for ourselves, that whenever we say, "Oh, you know I didn't mean it that way," or some such thing, we might be the part of the problem. Let's err on the side of learning more about what constitutes sexual harassment, and call it when we see it.

BATHROOM WARS:
A SOLUTION IN SEARCH
OF A PROBLEM
February 9, 2017

"We know it's going to be a tough fight. The forces of fear and misinformation will pull out all the stops, both in Texas and nationally. But we know we're on the right side of the issue, and we're on the right side of history."

These were Lieutenant Governor Dan Patrick's words a few weeks ago regarding the "bathroom wars," the debate about the use of school and public bathrooms by those who identify as transgender. The issue has moved from the headlines to the legislative agenda. The issue seemed to disappear for a while. It was not mentioned in the governor's State of the State address. But here it comes again.

Oh, the power of one's perspective. The forces of fear and misinformation are indeed at work, but not as Mr. Patrick describes. Political, cultural, and religious history reveal that history is on the side of inclusivity, justice, and compassion, not Mr. Patrick's divisive values and goals.

Those who identify as transgender or have family members who identify in that way already face discrimination, harassment, emotional and sometimes physical suffering. Those things come with being identified as transgender in this society. This is a result of misinformation, or lack of information. Now they also have to deal with the political bias of a zealous lieutenant governor who clearly has done little reading, studying or talking with those who will be most affected by his agenda.

As was true in North Carolina, this is a solution in search of a problem. In fact, it is a solution that will cause far more problems than the one it supposedly is trying to fix.

Mr. Patrick and those in the state house who are equally zealous to show how hard they are working to protect their constituents need to be clear about their focus. Keeping men out of girls' bathrooms, the fearful scenario always used, is not a transgender problem. That's a heterosexual predator problem. Call the police!

If there is a problem with providing transgender students, or any student for that matter, with a safe place for going to the bathroom, changing clothes, or showering after workouts, those are workable situations that do not require discriminatory or shaming legislation. Such solutions will require some thought, conversations with students, teachers, and school boards, and some planning. All of these are well within the capabilities of schools and school boards, and even some legislators.

Of course, the big impact of such unwise legislation will be economic. As North Carolina has experienced, Texas will suffer significant loss of revenue. If this legislation passes, it will eventually be repealed for the economic reasons, not the human rights reasons. Of course, an additional consequence to passing this legislation is that Texans will get the snickers, eye rolls, and head shaking from the rest of the country that until now have been reserved for North Carolina.

Mr. Patrick, you are not on the right side of the issue or the right side of history. You are on the side of fear, of closing ranks, of tightening restrictions on those you do not understand. The arc of history bends in the direction of justice, compassion, and inclusion.

IT'S NOT ABOUT
THE BATHROOM
May 22, 2016

You very likely have shared a public bathroom with a person who identifies as transgender. It probably went like this. You did your business. The other person did theirs. You left. They left. We already share public facilities and nothing happens.

I admit that I know little of the transgender world, but I do know that being transgender is a biological reality, not a choice. People do not switch genders because they feel like it. Arguing that a man could go into the women's bathroom because "I feel like a woman today" is merely intended to scare people. If someone does that, call the police. He's a heterosexual predator.

People who identify as transgender have been with us forever. Only recently have we begun to take their situation seriously. As we the public began taking them seriously, lawmakers got nervous and singled them out as targets for their agenda.

The "Religious Freedom" acts, allowing people to withhold services based on the customer's sexual orientation, and the "bathroom wars" requiring a person to use the bathroom that matches the gender on their birth certificate, are the most recent attempts by legislators to make a point, not to make a difference. The point is their disagreement with the legalization of same-sex marriage and other civil rights granted to LGBT citizens. These are efforts to circumvent the laws and maintain state sanctioned discrimination in the name of Christian values.

Some in the Texas legislature want to enlist in the bathroom wars. Lieutenant Governor Dan Patrick said, "This isn't about equal rights. This isn't about being against anyone or anti-any person. This is about common sense."

"Common sense" is a code word for simple, and this issue is anything but simple. Being transgender is certainly not simple, and finding a respectful response is not simple.

In some situations, common sense would be to use the bathroom that matches the gender on the birth certificate. In other situations this would grossly inappropriate. A person identifying as transgender could be a fourth grader just discovering that the body she was born with does not match who she is. Being transgender might also be a young adult undergoing hormone treatments who now finds their body somewhere between their birth gender and their new gender. The plumbing may be original, but it does not match the rest of the body. A transgender person might also be the guy who sits on the same aisle at church, whose kid plays on the same baseball team as your kid, whom you would never guess was born female. There is no simple, single, "common sense" response.

Of course, everyone wants to avoid the obvious problems. I don't want my daughter sharing a bathroom with someone who was born female but now, because of hormone treatments and surgery, is an adult male. I don't want a woman who was born a boy but has been female for the past two decades to come into my bathroom. And I certainly do not want children and teenagers singled out, harassed, or beaten up because they can no longer keep a personal situation private.

The real danger in public bathrooms is not from the person who is transgender but from heterosexual predators, straight men, women, boys, and girls who have problems with their perception, judgment, and impulse control.

We need to make accommodations. Some will involve money and effort. Mostly, though, we need to make an emotional and spiritual shift. As a culture we still have trouble taking in the stranger we do not understand. Our typical strategy is to avoid. If we can't avoid, we ostracize. When that no longer works, we use intimidation and hostility. Legislation is our most sophisticated strategy. Ironically, the legislators most likely to push these kinds of measures are the very ones who generally seek to limit government's intrusion in our lives.

Our lack of understanding breeds fear, and fear leads to hostility. Whether physical or legislative, it is the same frightened response toward those who are far more vulnerable than the ones making the rules. We could save ourselves a lot of time, trouble, and hypocrisy, and we could save lives, if we first sought to understand.

People who identify as transgender need our support, not our hostility. Undergoing the steps needed to make the change from their physiology at birth to a physiology that matches their identity requires courage, patience, and significant expense. The vast majority of individuals who identify as transgender have no interest in making trouble or even being noticed as transgender. They mostly want to live their lives, do their jobs, have families and friends, and enjoy what the rest of us take for granted.

HISTORY:
FACT AND PERSPECTIVE
June 3, 2013

"George Washington was a traitor." The whole class was stunned. How could a teacher of American history say such a thing? After a long pause, he followed with, "He was considered a traitor by the British."

That moment did not occur during an era of political correctness, nor did it happen in some liberal northern state. This happened during my 8th grade year in East Texas in the mid 60's. The teacher was as old as the hills. I remember that moment because something clicked inside me. History is not just about facts. It's not just about names and dates and places. History is also, and perhaps more so, about perspective. And perspective is not so much about being right and proving someone else wrong. It is about appreciating history from my experience and vantage point, and recognizing that the same history may be quite different from another's experience and vantage point.

Appreciating multiple perspectives is a mark of cognitive complexity and emotional maturity. By middle school, and certainly by high school, students should be able to consider history and social issues from more than a single perspective. Unfortunately that level of maturity and complexity appears to have eluded Texas Senator Daniel Patrick and his colleagues who have headed the effort to do away with CSCOPE, the computer-based curriculum used across the state at every grade level.

Opponents of CSCOPE cite several items in the curriculum that supposedly promote un-American and un-Christian perspectives. One such example presents the actions of those who threw British tea into Boston Harbor in 1773. Their actions are described without historical context and without reference to who did it and to whom it was done. Students are then asked to evaluate whether or not the actions constituted terrorism.

With more than 200 years of American history to reflect on, we know that the Boston Tea Party was a pivotal event in the revolution that ultimately led to our independence from Great Britain. From an American perspective these were actions of patriots, not terrorists. Yet, the action was not universally acceptable even to citizens and leaders of the American Revolution, some of whom considered it unwise to destroy property and break laws even for a righteous cause. To the British, of course, it was an act of treason. So was this an act of terrorism or an act of defiance for a good cause? Is it only considered terrorism if you are the target? It depends on your perspective, which is precisely how high school students should be thinking.

Education should and must go beyond the conveyance of facts and figures. Education must be concerned with nurturing inquisitive minds, encouraging critical thinking, and developing the capacity to see and appreciate multiple perspectives. Otherwise we are depriving our children of a skill that is increasingly necessary in today's pluralistic society and global community.

American values, Christian values, and Texas values cannot be singular, provincial, and simplistic. Limiting our perspective to only what we are familiar and comfortable with produces a narrow and skewed view of the world.

If our goal is for students to internalize and appreciate their history and values, they must learn to carefully consider and weigh those values against other worthwhile ideas. Otherwise we're left with well-rehearsed bumper-sticker beliefs that may or may not make a difference in our behavior.

Sadly, the legislators who led the charge to drop CSCOPE have violated some important conservative values to accomplish their purpose. CSCOPE provided a common curriculum across most of the state and allowed local school districts and individual teachers to customize their curriculum to the students with whom they work. Dropping CSCOPE without the consultation of educators and school administrators sends the message that local school districts and individual teachers are not to be trusted to know their own students and to make appropriate educational choices on their behalf. Control is given instead to a small group of state bureaucrats, most of whom I suppose are not comfortable with complex thought and multiple perspectives.

CHURCH AND POLITICS

Christianity is political. However, Christianity does not belong to one party. Democrats and Republicans mix religion and politics as long as the result supports their cause. However, doing so leads to a convoluted and diluted Christianity as well as government that discriminates on "religious" grounds.

Religious leaders, politicians, and people of faith must always remember that a legislative, executive, or judicial solution to a social or political problem will never be the Christian response. An institutional response, whether it's a government, business, church, or social club will always focus on what is best for the institution. A Christian response will always focus on what best serves the needs of the ones who are most adversely affected by the situation. The institution will always seek to maintain its power structure. A Christian response will see the power structure as part of the problem.

WHAT IS A CHRISTIAN RESPONSE
TO A POLITICAL CRISIS?
July 21, 2019

The parable of the Good Samaritan was one of the suggested texts from the church lectionary this past Sunday. Most churchgoers know the story from Luke's gospel of the unlikely helper of the guy who was attacked, beaten, and left for dead in the ditch.

"Who is my neighbor?" is the question raised by this story, and the question couldn't be more timely, yet still ambiguous. Social surveys show we know fewer of our logistical neighbors today than in generations past. Yet digitally we are connected to "friends" all over the world that we may never meet face to face. We get instantaneous news from the other side of the globe, but we often don't know about the heartbreak next door.

Three contemporary issues stand out for me in this story. First, the traveler was making his journey alone. That made him vulnerable to attack. We are more vulnerable to emotional distress or to being exploited when we feel alone. And ironically, nothing causes us to feel more alone than being vulnerable. Bullies know that. Child predators and scam artists know that. Life seems to conspire against us when we feel alone.

Second, the traveler ended up in the ditch through no fault of his own. He was simply going about his business, traveling from point A to point B. We still tend to get caught up in faulty thinking that because something bad happened, he must have brought it on himself. We blame the victim because it makes us feel safer. Experience teaches us that, contrary to our simple but faulty logic, it's never that simple. Bad things happen to good people. In fact, bad things happen to all people.

Tragedies and disasters happen to people all the time through no fault of their own. Good, healthy people die of undeserved, horrible diseases every day. Bad things happen, period. Sometimes we end up in the ditch like the man in the parable because that's how life happens.

And in the same way that the person in the ditch was not there because of some evil, those on the road were not there because of their righteousness. Most of the time, life and circumstance put us where we are, on the road or in the ditch, through no fault or goodness of our own.

It is a matter of complex circumstance that one person is in the ditch and one person is on the road. And it's probably only a matter of time until they switch places.

And finally, this parable speaks to the humanitarian crisis on the border that, according to this parable, involves our neighbors. Jesus could not have predicted the nature of our world today, but he could not have told a more relevant or timely story.

The political blaming and posturing keep taking the spotlight away from the immigration crisis itself, but there are people in the ditch in desperate need, and we who are on the road, supposedly following Jesus' example, have choices to make.

This crisis requires a legislative solution AND a Christian response. However, we should never confuse the two. A legislative solution or an executive order can never be the same as a Christian response.

Any institutional response will focus on what is best for the institution. Whether the institution is a government, a global business, a church or university, or a small family enterprise, institutions will always focus on keeping the institution intact and strong. That's how they keep going.

But that is not a Christian approach. In the face of human suffering, Jesus always came down on the side of the person or people most adversely affected by the situation. He stood with the people who had no access to political or financial power. He referred to them as "the least of these."

Political interventions are necessary, but we should never assume that any political decision is also the spiritual one. The institution will not see the face of the person in the ditch. The institution, by its nature, will focus on alleviating the inconvenience caused by the person in the ditch.

The Christian response is to see the face of the person in the ditch, to be a neighbor to that person, even the person we fear. That's what Jesus told us to do. We do it also because it is only a matter of time until we are the one in the ditch and in need of just such a neighbor.

OUT OF CHAOS, CLARITY?
July 27, 2017

Out of the chaos will come clarity. At least that is my hope.

Amidst the incendiary rhetoric, ongoing investigations, incessant legal and ethical crises, accusations, lying, and blaming for all that's not working, the chaos of Donald Trump's administration may provide some important clarification for us as a nation.

The Donald will not be the clarifier. He is the catalyst, creating the refining fire of our identity as a nation. We, the American people, will be forced to clarify who we are and who we want to be in the days ahead.

One sobering clarification for us church-going, Bible-believing folks of West Texas is that America is not a Christian nation. We have never been, but now it is obvious. For just one example, David Brooks of the New York Times quoted a Wall Street Journal article by two of Trump's top advisors. "The president embarked on his first foreign trip with a clear-eyed outlook that the world is not a 'global community' but an arena where nations, nongovernmental actors and businesses engage and compete for advantage."

Brooks went on to write, "This sentence is the epitome of the Trump project. It asserts that selfishness is the sole driver of human affairs. It grows out of a worldview that life is a competitive struggle for gain. It implies that cooperative communities are hypocritical covers for the selfish jockeying underneath."

This is an articulate version of "American First," a simple political slogan that should be a flashing red light to all Christians.

We are a nation made up predominantly of people who identify as Christian. That's a fact. But that does not constitute a "Christian nation." A Christian nation implies a nation guided by principles and values of Jesus Christ, not just an affiliation. Yet, those of us who identify as Christian would never vote for a candidate at any level whose platform is the Beatitudes, who promises to "seek first the kingdom of God," to love our enemies, and to turn the other cheek.

This is not a condemnation of Christianity or of our nation. This is an acknowledgement that frees us to be patriotic citizens who also recognize the inherent conflicts of being a citizen of this country and a follower of Jesus. They are not synonymous. They aren't even compatible most of the time. When we try to make them compatible, we abandoned the teachings of Jesus.

So what might this mean for those of us who are Christians? For one thing, it means we have to pay attention to the presence or absence of Christian principles in policies being proposed. For example, the budget and healthcare decisions are each moral issues being treated as though they are merely financial decisions. Like many others, I get caught up in the question, "How will this affect me?" The moral, Christian question is, "How will this affect the least of these?"

How we limit or expand vital services, basic care, and access to a dignified life for the most needy among us says much more about those of us who have enough than it does about those in deepest need.

The current chaos will force us to clarify who we are and who we want to become in many other areas, such as immigration, education, the role of science in our decision-making, and our role with other nations of the world. Each of these provides the opportunity to close ranks, build walls, and take care of our own, or to take seriously the words engraved on the Statue of Liberty and spoken in the Sermon on the Mount.

Trump's election was assisted by many who were angry about the current system and who felt left behind economically. The question now is, will we as a nation of conservatives, moderates, and liberals continue to be driven by anger and fear about our personal situations or will we realize we are in this together and our concerns must extend to the larger community and global community, and yes, even to our enemies, however we choose to define them.

In a recent opinion article in the Reporter News, the writer stated that we cannot vote based on a candidate's character. "Choices must be based on the issues." I wholeheartedly disagree.

Issues come and go, issues get redefined, simplified, and complicated. Our opinions change as we change and grow. I prefer to vote based on character as demonstrated in a leader's long-term commitments and behaviors over time, not on something they say on a particular day to garner support.

We are not a Christian nation, but we can be a nation in which character and Christian values matter. More than party, opinions, or policies in the long run.

PRAY FOR RAIN
August 10, 2014

"Pray for Rain." The sign in the front yard expressed the wishes of lots of folks in this part of the country. We need rain. Living without cell phones, gasoline, or electricity would be tough, but these are optional. Water is not. In that same yard, however, the sprinkler system was pumping about 60 gallons of water per minute, much of which, by the time I came walking by, was running down the street.

These signs appear to be a demonstration of faith, suggesting hope and faith that God will respond to our petition with the desired result: rain. However, prayers for rain also reveal an inherent contradiction in our beliefs about such prayers.

The belief that a fervent prayer will produce the desired outcome is based on the assumption that God controls or manages events, including the weather, and can be persuaded to act in response to our prayers. The Bible appears to suggest as much. We ask God to alter the course of a disease when we don't want someone to die. We ask God to keep a loved one safe on a trip, which implies changing the road conditions or driving habits of others. We pray for wisdom at the beginning of a business meeting so that things will go the right way. That's one side of faith, the self-serving side that expresses our wishes.

However, if we believe, either from a creationist perspective or a scientific perspective, that God is in some way in charge of the heavens and the earth, and we believe that the created or existing order is as God ordained it to be, then a prayer for rain essentially is a questioning of God's judgment and asking for a change in how things are done.

Praying for rain seems to be saying, "Even though we trust that you are in charge of things, God, and we trust that you know what you are doing, we're not too happy with how your system is working. It is causing us some distress, and we want you to modify things on our behalf. We'd like for you to make things better for us."

Ironically and tragically, in other parts of the country and the world, people are busy praying for the rains to subside before their houses are washed away.

Any God that can be convinced to change things on our behalf is a God unworthy of our worship. We should be wary of a God who will modify the national weather patterns for our benefit and convenience while so many others in the world have no clean water, no food, or are fleeing their country in fear with nothing more than what they can carry.

This is the same mentality displayed by a person who walks away from a serious accident saying, "God must have been with me," the implication being that for the person who was injured or killed, God was nowhere to be found. Those of us who have lived long enough know that life and God don't work that way.

It seems to me that a truly faithful stance would be to pray for wisdom and patience and resourcefulness in the midst of a situation we do not understand and is completely out of our control. If we believe God is in charge of things, our task should be to learn what we can from the draught, to discover what our role in the draught might be, to do everything in our power to be responsible stewards of the water we have, and to make a long-term plan in case the draught from God persists. In fact, praying for forgiveness for squandering our resources seems a better start than praying for rain.

When interviewed by a reporter at last year's community prayer meeting for rain, a local minister said something more truthful than he probably intended. "If we don't get rain soon, we'll have to change our lifestyle."

Changing our lifestyle by becoming more conscious of and conservative in our use of water is completely within our control, and it seems the spiritually responsible thing to do. It is the very least we can do, literally.

So continue to pray, but while you are praying, take some actions that may make a difference while we wait for rain. Perhaps our signs should read, "While we pray for rain, let's conserve water."

CHRISTIAN CONTORTIONISTS
July 10, 2016

Donald Trump is on a campaign to win over conservative Christians. This would be laughable except that Christian conservatives appear to be buying it. Even James Dobson testified that Trump, who recently stated he had nothing to confess to God because he didn't do many bad things, is now a "baby Christian."

This particular sideshow is not so much about Donald Trump, but about how, once again, this presidential campaign is forcing Christians to become spiritual contortionists.

Four years ago, Robert Jeffress, senior pastor of First Baptist Church of Dallas, stated during the Republican primary that he could never endorse the member of a cult. He was referring, of course, to Mitt Romney, a Mormon. Once Romney became the candidate, though, Jeffress endorsed him wholeheartedly over a devout Christian, but a Democrat. The circus "rubber man" would have been proud.

The same thing is happening this time around, putting many conservative Christians in a quandary. A Republican endorsement, generally a no-brainer with evangelicals, is now an endorsement of someone who embodies all manner of things evangelicals abhor. If Trump were a Democrat, conservative Christians would be planning a preemptive impeachment rather than trying to figure out how to vote for him without really endorsing him.

Spiritual contortions. We all do this to justify actions, beliefs, and prejudices that we know, beyond all doubt, are counter to who we want to be. We mentally bend and twist and gyrate until we can rationalize whatever we need to.

Trump is helping evangelical contortionists to sleep well at night by saying what they want to hear. It matters not if he means what he says, or even understands what he says. He is saying the right things, though awkwardly, but in this case, having almost the right language will substitute for genuine faith. He's a salesman after all, and his evangelical bandwagon is filling up.

Most versions of Christianity we hear on the campaign trail are patriotic American-style versions, with little or no resemblance to what we read in the gospels. Every candidate at the local, state, and national level hopes he or she can sound "Christian enough" to garner support.

What's a good Christian to do? Must we think? Pay attention?

My suggestion is that we not have a Christian president. Well, maybe the president could be Christian, but we shouldn't know it until after the election. Prior to the election, candidates may not talk about their faith. The candidates may only talk about what they have done and about their vision for the country. They can cover all the topics we need to hear about to make an informed decision, but they may not trot God out as if they have had a divine revelation or have received a divine endorsement. Then, if Christians want to make a "Christian choice," they can decide which person's words and actions are most in line with the teachings and example of Jesus.

Can you imagine someone espousing a true Christian message during the campaign? Someone committed to living and governing according to the words and example of Jesus would never survive a primary, and certainly not the presidency. How long would a candidate last who is truly meek, who seeks to be a peacemaker, who would not retaliate but instead turn the other cheek? What would happen in a debate to the one who insisted that as a country we love our enemies, even the ones who are trying to kill us, and that we humble ourselves, repent, and seek first the kingdom of God above all the trade agreements and homeland security policies. And what would a candidate say about the economy and caring for the poor from a Christ-like perspective?

I doubt I would vote for a candidate who presented that political agenda. As Christians we must stop rationalizing our vote as "the Christian choice." If we want to cast a Christian vote, we must do our homework. We must ask tough questions and not settle for bumper sticker answers. Then we must vote for the person whose demonstrated ethics and worldview align most with our nation's history of protecting freedom, seeking justice, and insuring the inclusion and well-being of everyone, not just the ones like us. If that person then happens to be a Christian, fine.

BLURRING THE LINES BETWEEN
CHURCH AND STATE
October 12, 2014

Religion is declining in its influence in America according to nearly three quarters of those surveyed in a recent Pew Research poll. Most thought that was a bad thing.

In the same poll, nearly half of those surveyed indicated that churches and houses of worship should express their views on social and political issues, and a growing number, though still a minority, thought churches should endorse candidates for political office. Those who were affiliated with a church were more supportive of politicians talking more about religion.

One person on a FOX News team summed up this report by saying, "People today are scared." I don't know if that is the motivation behind the views of those surveyed, but it is consistent with what happens when we get scared.

When we get scared, we don't want information. We want comfort, assurance, and guidance. We turn to the people we already trust, and we become more skeptical of the people we are already have doubts about. Of course, this leaves us wide open to the biases of those we trust and we miss the wisdom of those who have a different opinion.

Fortunately, many religious leaders stay informed on political and social issues and can help their congregations address the issues and fears from a broad perspective. However, many other religious leaders approach the issues from a strict doctrinal perspective or from their own personal bias. Too often then, people are simply told what they should think, do, or believe.

As a seminary student, one of my biggest disappointments was being taught **what** to think about particular issues and **what** to believe about scripture and doctrine. There was little emphasis on **how** to think about those things. I was not encouraged to ask critical questions nor to look at issues from a variety of Biblical or historical perspectives or even through the lens of my own personal perspective, all of which should play into any commitment or statement of belief. In short, I was taught to be a good minister, not a good thinker.

Should churches and ministers address social and political issues? Absolutely. However, they should do so not by instructing people on what to think or how to respond to a particular issue, but rather by encouraging people to think fully and clearly about issues, and by providing them opportunities to discuss those issues together.

Church leaders and congregations should have the goal of helping one another to carefully and prayerfully consider all sides of an issue, to discuss with and listen openly to those who have different experiences and perspectives, to consider the many individuals who are affected, and to filter our responses through Jesus' example of compassion and inclusion. We should be encouraged to ask all the questions we can of each other and of our leaders, because it is in the questions and the discussion that truth is found. Not in declarations. Wanting our political leaders to talk about religious things is a steeper and more slippery slope. Our elected officials don't have to have an ounce of religious conviction or spiritual guidance in order to invoke the name of God in their speeches. Yet, we Christians are gullible and tend to believe and follow the ones who do use God language, regardless of their motivation. Likewise, we distrust those who don't use God language.

If elected officials are going to invoke the name of God in their speeches, we should ask what they mean by that. The third commandment, the prohibition about taking God's name in vain, has nothing to do with cursing. It has everything to do with using God's name to curry the favor of others for one's own agenda.

These research trends appear to stand in contradiction to the constitutional right we know as "the separation of church and state." If Christians choose to blur those lines, we must at least be well informed. We must listen respectfully to those whose views are different and be open to taking a position that follows Jesus' example, even though doing so may contradict the views of the institutional church. An open heart and open mind rarely follow the institutional path.

THE WAR ON CHRISTMAS
December 2, 2007

Now that Thanksgiving and Black Friday have come and gone, the Christmas season is in high gear. And so is the battle over Christmas. I have already received emails asking me to support causes combatting those pesky atheists and/or civil libertarians who want to take religion out of the holiday season. Christians are voicing their objection about advertisers and store clerks substituting "Happy Holidays" for "Merry Christmas." Some small town will once again make national news when they are ordered by the court to remove a manger scene from the courthouse lawn or drop a third-grade Christmas pageant.

"Keep Christ in Christmas" will be the battle cry among the Christian faithful who even criticized George Bush last year for leaving Christ out of the White House Christmas card. Meanwhile, others will continue efforts to remove Christian symbols, stories, and songs from public celebrations and displays. Some of these efforts are out of respect for people of other faiths, many of whom also have their own religious holidays at this time of year. Others stand on the principle of separation of church and state. The battle is on between those who want to keep Christ either in or out of the holidays.

The problem is we are trying to celebrate two different holidays. They coincide on the calendar and go by the same name, "Christmas," but they couldn't be more different.

One holiday is the religious celebration of the birth of Jesus, the one whose life is the basis of our faith. Advent, a four-week period preceding Christmas, promotes spiritual preparation for the day of celebration.

The religious celebration of Christmas, however, has little to do with the other concurrent holiday, the commercial and cultural Christmas. This holiday is, well, commercial and cultural. The focus is on buying and selling, giving and getting. Our nation's economic well-being, as well as the survival of some of our largest retailers, hinge on the public spending heavily during this season. This year's spending is projected to be about $900 per person.

Christmas is also cultural, transcending national and even religious boundaries. Many songs of the season warm our hearts but have nothing to do with the birth of Jesus. Family rituals and gatherings serve as anchors in our personal histories, but again, many such gatherings have no basis in the religious celebration.

So how do we resolve this battle over Christmas? Shall we try to merge these different celebrations, to make the commercial Christmas more religious or visa versa? Shall we separate them even more? I think the latter would serve us all better.

Christians should do everything in their power to make Advent and Christmas a truly sacred season that is unique to our spiritual heritage. Christians should not look to the government to support their celebration of Christmas. That's not the job of government. Retail stores should not be expected to support the religious holiday. They are not in business for that purpose.

When Christians more clearly distinguish the religious holiday from the commercial one, we can craft sacred events and rituals that remind us of the humble and frightening beginnings of our faith. Then, if we want to join others in celebrating the cultural and commercial holiday season, we can do so with great joy. We can join the predawn stampedes on Black Friday, we can shop 'til we drop, and we can wish everyone "Happy Holidays," because we are addressing the weightier spiritual matters in our own way.

Merry Christmas AND Happy Holidays!

UNDERSTANDING LAGS
BEHIND EXPERIENCE
May 20, 2012

*Written 3 years before the Supreme Court
legalized same-sex marriage in all states.*

When my son was a teenager, he stayed out one night about 3 hours past his curfew. This was unusual, because even though he was pretty headstrong in most things, he was usually dutiful when it came to curfew. Intuition, though, told me not to worry about him that night. However, I did wait up, and when he came in, we talked.

"I'm sorry, Dad, but I just had to. There's a lot going on, and I was going to go crazy if I didn't do something." He provided few details other than that he had been talking with friends, but the feelings he conveyed struck a deep chord of memory in me. He had to violate the current norms in order to respond to a deeper sense of what he needed, and he was willing to risk my disapproval and possible punishment to do it.

There's always a space between what we know deep inside and what we are able to articulate. Often we must act without fully understanding why we are doing what we are doing. Understanding always seems to lag behind experience, and that lag time can be confusing and even paralyzing.

One reason for the lag time is that a new realization of what's right and true usually violates some past definition of what was right and true at the time.

I think that is what is at work today following President Obama's announcement that he personally supports same-sex marriage. He reported a few years ago that his views on the matter were "evolving" and we've all had an uncomfortable lag time to talk, worry, lobby, debate, and even pass preemptive legislation. This lag time will no doubt continue as we wait to see how this plays out. In fact, his announcement will likely further polarize us on this issue.

But the arc of history has been moving in the direction of legalizing same-sex marriage, and our president has now made that direction public.

What he and many other advocates have recognized is that the issue of same-sex marriage is no longer an issue of morality but rather an issue of civil rights. For many it is still a moral issue, but for a slight majority of the population now, this is a matter of equal rights and a cessation of discrimination. That is the shift; from what we once thought to be right to what we are now coming to understand.

For generations this has been an uncontested moral issue. Homosexuality was "in the closet" for good reasons. We did not understand it. We attached layers of stigma to the few who chose to be open about their homosexuality. Because it looked like a rare phenomenon, we were comfortable considering it an aberration. The medical and mental health communities considered it a disorder. But we now know more. Our medical, genetic, and behavioral research has given us more information. And as human beings, it seems that as our mind expands, so does our inclusion.

What we discover to be right and true at a deep personal level takes a while to become public, even longer to become social, and then a matter of policy. But the direction seems set. What is right at a deep level for our president and for a growing number of people in this country is to provide the same rights, responsibilities, and privileges to people who wish to marry someone of their same sex as we do to those who marry someone of the other sex.

Churches and denominations will weigh in on this, and should do so. The voice of religion is crucial in any social issue. But this has now become a matter of civil law and civil rights, not Biblical interpretation.

I suspect that one day, our children or grandchildren's generation will say the same thing we now say about some of the social conflicts of past generations, "I can't believe you used to fight about that."

BEHAVIOR IS A CHOICE,
SEXUAL ORIENTATION IS NOT

March 1, 2008

*Written 7 years before the Supreme Court
legalized same-sex marriage in every state.*

Same-sex marriage remains a volatile issue. While society struggles to clarify the implications and legal ramifications of same-sex marriage, some churches debate whether or not homosexuality is a sin and whether or not gays and lesbians have a place in church leadership, or even in membership. The legal and civil rights of same-sex couples become clouded when homosexuality is also argued to be a moral issue. These are important concerns, and it's gratifying to see the newspaper allowing dialogue through guest editorials and letters.

In a recent editorial, one writer made an important point. Same-sex marriage is a legal matter, not a religious one. Churches may conduct and bless marriages, and congregations may accept or refuse same-sex partners within their membership. However, the church should have no say about whether or not a same-sex couple can file jointly on their income tax, share health benefits, make end of life decisions for each other, or any of the other legal privileges now shared by heterosexual couples only. In our society, marriage is a legal status.

The article, however, went on to make two distinctions that seem simplistic and therefore cloud the issues. The first distinction is made between "Bible believers" who see homosexuality as a sin and "everyone else" who sees homosexuality as acceptable. As a "Bible believer" I do not share the author's views. There are scriptures that, when read literally and without attention to the culture and worldview of that time, do condemn homosexual acts. When read literally and selectively, it is easy enough to find scriptures to condemn almost anything you wish to condemn, and to support those things you wish to support.

There are other hermeneutically sound ways of reading, interpreting, and applying the Bible that do not lead to such exclusionary conclusions. There are also many who are not "Bible believers" who condemn homosexuality for reasons other than what it says in scripture.

The article also suggests that homosexuality is "either a legitimate choice or an innate compulsion." This grossly oversimplifies sexual orientation. Behavior is a choice, whether heterosexual or homosexual. Sexual orientation is not. If we are to see sexual orientation as a choice, then we must also ask questions such as, "How did you decide you wanted to be heterosexual?" or "When did you choose to be attracted to people of the opposite sex?" The other option provided is "innate compulsion." "Innate?" Yes. Sexual orientation is part of who the person is. It is part of their biological and neurological make-up. "Compulsion?" No more or less than heterosexuality is a compulsion. Again, behavior can be compulsive, but orientation is not.

When the church can acknowledge sexual orientation, whether heterosexual or homosexual, as a natural part of a person's complex identity, we can abandon the condescending sentiment, "Love the sinner, hate the sin." This communicates pity. I suspect that individuals who are gay or lesbian need what each of us needs, acceptance and compassion, not pity.

Christian churches should be leading the way in promoting full acceptance of those marginalized in our culture. That was the example Jesus set. Instead, while denominations are splitting over whether or not gays and lesbians have a place in the church, many businesses are moving forward with non-discriminatory policies and same-sex partner benefits. Devoted Christians who are gay or lesbian not only have to deal with cultural stigma, but many have to do it without the support of their church. When businesses are more compassionate than churches, something is amiss.

Anne Lamott warns, "You can safely assume you've created God in your own image when it turns out that God hates all the same people you do." I fear this is true for us when we use the law or the scriptures to exclude those we fear or abhor.

"CONSERVATIVE CHRISTIAN"
SHOULD NOT BE A CAMPAIGN SLOGAN
April 17, 2016

Now that the presidential candidates are no longer campaigning in the South and Southwest, they are touting their Christian credentials far less often. Sure, there are Christians in other parts of the country, but the label is less salient as a demographic descriptor elsewhere than it is here in West Texas.

Around here, it's huge. In the recent local primaries, for example, candidates for practically every office listed "Conservative Christian" as one of their selling points. This label was used in conjunction with other predictable descriptors, such as Pro-Life, Defender of the Second Amendment, and anti-immigration. There was little to distinguish one from another, including religious affiliation.

I get concerned when "Conservative Christian" or "Evangelical Christian" is used as a campaign label, particularly when it is casually grouped with other political positions as if they were synonymous. They are not.

Being Christian is not a simple or monolithic position. For some, being Christian is simply an affiliation, belonging to a particular congregation or denomination. Most of us were born into Christian families and we grew up in predominantly Christian communities. Being a Christian was in the baby food we ate. We may claim we are Christian by choice, but where I grew up, it was the only choice.

For others, to be a Christian is to make a conscious decision, coupled with a personally held set of beliefs. Yet, even that is not simple or singular. The differences in the decisions and beliefs among even people who sit in the same worship service are sometimes dramatic. What it means to be a Christian varies widely among believers who supposedly hold common beliefs.

Still others consider Christianity to be attitudinal and behavioral rather than by affiliation or doctrine. Living a Christ-like life is what counts. "By their fruits you will know them."

In short, being Christian is not a singular or simple matter, so when someone struts Christianity as a political label, I want to know what that means to them.

Watching candidates competing for the evangelical vote is like watching someone compete for "most humble." It is grossly contradictory to what it means to be Christian for many of us. How can someone essentially be voted "most popular" among people whose lives should be characterized by humility, sacrifice, service, and "dying to self"?

Likewise, equating "Conservative Christian" with issues that involve insuring my rights is antithetical to the teachings of Jesus. Insuring your own rights or the rights of those who are like you may be patriotic, but it is not necessarily Christian.

In the same way that candidates simplify Christianity, they also simplify social and moral issues. Doing so allows candidates to more easily merge the issues with their Christian credentials. Even complex issues like abortion, rights of same-sex marriages, or immigration are artificially simplified by seeing them through a single perspective, such as a denomination or a political party.

Yet, aren't we as Christians encouraged to view these matters with attention to how the most vulnerable will be affected? When viewed as complex issues that have different consequences for each group affected, there is no simple Christian response that Republicans or Democrats can claim as their own.

As a voting public, it does not serve us well to simplify the issues and to assume that our group has the final truth of the matter. When I assume I have the final truth, I leave no room for anything new. No room for new information, no possibility that someone else may possess a truth I might learn from, and no room for compassion for those who hold a different view.

There are theological and political implications when we do so. Politically, we are left with hateful rhetoric, entrenchment, and stalemate on issues that deserve our best and most compassionate efforts. Theologically we are left with an anemic Christianity that is shaped by the latest campaign drama or political personality rather than by the teachings of Jesus and the real needs of the world around us.

THE PARADOX OF FREEDOM
AND RESPONSIBILITY
April 14, 2013

Big sodas live on in New York City. Mayor Blumberg's attempt to ban large sugary drinks in the city was overturned by a state court. For now. The Mayor promises to appeal. The interesting thing about all this has been the range of reactions. Some shrug and say, "Makes sense." Others are furious.

Banning big sugary drinks provides an amusing focus for the far greater issues at work: balancing personal freedom with social responsibility and determining the role of government in regulating that balance. This is not a new debate. Remember the turmoil over smoking in public places, wearing seat belts, and limiting the size of shampoo bottle we can carry onboard an airplane?

Now we are dealing with questions of voter identification, immigration reform, health care reform, marriage equality, just to name a few.

For some, establishing common sense guidelines for the sale, purchase, and ownership of firearms and ammunition rises to the level of a constitutional right, and many scream that it therefore cannot be limited. Of course it can be limited. It already has been. There are some weapons you cannot legally purchase or own.

Just as the freedom of speech and assembly and protection from unlawful search and seizure require refinement, definition, and appropriate boundaries for the sake of the common good, so does the right to bear arms.

All of these issues require our judicial system interpreting the Constitution in ways that balance personal freedom and public responsibility in an increasingly complex world.

These matters are complicated because none of these is an either/or argument. Balancing freedom and responsibility is a both/and paradox. Both sides of the argument appear to be contradictory, but each is true. When we ignore either side of a paradox, we inevitably find ourselves at an impasse.

This became clearest to while raising my children. Each parent wants to nurture and protect their children from harm AND they want to promote experiences that will help their children grow. Sometimes those goals are at odds, because many of our most important growth come from experiences of disappointment, loss, risk, and failure. Protecting our children from life's harshness AND allowing them to grow from life's harshness is a parent's job. It's not either/or. It's both/and, how much, and when.

Our country seems poised at that parental spot right now. We, including our legislators, are approaching issues such as gun regulation, marriage equality, women's reproductive rights, and even banning big sodas with an adolescent "either/or" mindset rather than an adult mind capable of dealing with complexity, contradiction, and paradox.

Like most people, I get worked up at those regulations that infringe on my freedom. I don't drink big sugary sodas, so shrugging that one off is easy for me. For others it's a huge deal. I roll my eyes at the limitations that don't make sense, and I get riled at those that infringe on something important to me. But none of those reactions includes the complexity of considering the greater good, and that greater good must be at least as important as my individual rights if we are to mature as a nation.

The preamble to the Constitution that guarantees our personal rights also includes the phrase, "to promote the general welfare." We are not a collection of individuals who share a national identity. We are a community, a society, a nation of people who must always ask, "How will this affect others?"

We live in a world that our founding fathers could never have imagined. We are more connected to small nations on the other side of globe than were contiguous states at the time our constitution was written. To imagine we can claim our personal freedoms without seriously considering our social responsibility, national implications, even global responsibility, is immature and irresponsible.

138